Classic Browns

CLASSIC CLEVELAND

Classic Browns: The 50 Greatest Games in Cleveland Browns History
JONATHAN KNIGHT

Classic Browns

THE 50 GREATEST GAMES IN CLEVELAND BROWNS HISTORY

Jonathan Knight

The Kent State University Press • Kent, Ohio

© 2008 by The Kent State University Press, Kent, Ohio 44242
All rights reserved.
Library of Congress Catalog Card Number 2008021130
ISBN 978-0-87338-986-0
Manufactured in the United States of America

Library of Congress Cataloging-in-Publication Data
Knight, Jonathan, 1976–
    Classic Browns : the 50 greatest games in Cleveland Browns history / by Jonathan Knight.
        p.   cm. — (Classic Cleveland)
    ISBN 978-0-87338-986-0 (pbk. : alk. paper) ∞
    1. Cleveland Browns (Football team : 1946–1995)—History. I. Title.
    GV956.C6K64 2008
    796.332'640977132—dc22   2008021130

British Library Cataloging-in-Publication data are available.

12 11 10 09 08   5 4 3 2 1

Dedicated to the next generation of Cleveland sports fans—

NEVER STOP BELIEVING.

Contents

"Just because it's ours why must it be worthless?"
—Esther Franz
from *The Price* by Arthur Miller

Preface

I can't tell you how many times over the past year this joke came flying at me like a flaming arrow in the night . . .

SOMEONE: Hey, what's your next book gonna be about?
ME: It's going to rank the fifty greatest games in Browns history.
SOMEONE: Have there been that many?
(Cue laugh track.)

But seriously, folks, that's what you hold in your hands: a countdown, constructed through perspective and research, of the greatest games in Cleveland Browns history. And yes, there have indeed been fifty. In fact, the deeper I delved into the project, the more I realized this collection could have easily swelled to 100 or more.

In my mind, any team that has played at least fifty games technically can have a list of its fifty greatest games. You don't have to earn the right. Granted, not all such countdowns would be that interesting to read. Baseball's Tampa Bay Rays, for instance, have been around for more than a decade and have yet to post a winning season. But even the Rays are entitled to a list of fifty greatest games. It wouldn't be that impressive, but with each subsequent addition and subtraction, the list would grow more meaningful and become more difficult to compile as the team's history grew richer. The Browns' list, conversely, *is* quite impressive and, hopefully, will be interesting to read—sort of a patchwork narrative of the team's enchanting history. That's one of the most wonderful things about sports: no matter how good or bad your team is, it has a history. And each game—good, bad, or ugly—is another chapter to that story. And, if we're lucky, it also becomes another memorable chapter in our own lives.

Accordingly, historical significance was the guidepost for this endeavor. Much like Deep Throat's cryptic guidance to Bob Woodward in *All the President's*

Men, I tried to "follow the history." There was no formula for determining this list, no scoring system designed to deem one game greater than another. To be sure, the majority of the games at the top of the list were generally playoffs or championships, hence giving them more weight. Nor does this list represent the fifty most *exciting* games the Browns have ever played. While I hope there's a natural parallel there, this list is based more on relevance than last-second field goals or fourth-quarter comebacks. Hopefully, each story will testify to its respective game's placement on the list and even if you don't agree with where it's been placed, you'll be able to appreciate why.

I certainly don't expect you to agree with each selection. There are games it simply broke my heart not to include. Conversely, there undoubtedly are contests on this list you'll feel don't belong. My mission is not to get you to concur, but rather to discuss. My hope is that this book—and the Indians and Cavaliers versions to follow—will launch debates across dinner tables and through commercial breaks for years to come. Maybe it can serve as a bridge between generations, further strengthening the bond of Cleveland's teams between parents and children who may not have too many other bonds to fall back upon. And in so doing, each time family or friends gather together to watch these beloved teams becomes its own wonderfully memorable moment.

For many longtime sports fans, significant moments in their lives and significant moments on the playing field become intertwined—with one making the other a bit more meaningful. For example, let me relate my own experience from the most recent game in this collection.

We flew to New England in September 2007 for a family wedding on a gorgeous bluff overlooking the Atlantic Ocean that made us all feel like the Kennedys gathering for a clambake at Hyannis Port. Naturally, with most of the guests from Cleveland, the flow of conversation eventually turned to the sorry state of the Browns, who were six days removed from an embarrassing opening-day loss to Pittsburgh and the twenty-two-minute Charlie Frye era at quarterback. With the Browns set to play Cincinnati—a team they always struggled with—the next day, the topic of discussion certainly wasn't whether the Browns could win. Everyone was guessing at what point in the game rookie quarterback Brady Quinn would take over for Charlie Frye–doppelganger Derek Anderson—and on a broader scale, whether head coach Romeo Crennel would last until Halloween.

Our flight back didn't take off until the next evening, so we had a few hours to kick around Boston on Sunday afternoon. My brother-in-law, wife, four-year-old son, and I decided to take a tour of Fenway Park, which, though it meant nothing at the time, began at 1 p.m.—the same time the Browns and Bengals were kicking off. As we followed our guide around the ballpark, listening to stories about the Red Sox and the haunted grounds they called home, something strange was going on in Cleveland. I first caught wind of it when I glanced at a television screen hanging in one of the empty Fenway concourses and saw the score. The Browns were winning, 20–14, in the second quarter. I was instantly puzzled. After what had happened the previous week, I didn't think the Browns would score twenty points all year. How could this be happening?

Just as we left Fenway, my son—who had been a trouper all weekend—fell asleep in my arms, and we began the long trek back across Beantown. As we left the park, we passed a sports bar hanging off the side of Fenway like a booger on a nightstand, and I caught a glimpse of the Browns game on one of the multiple televisions. It was almost halftime and now the Browns were up 27–21. I desperately needed answers. This couldn't be the doing of this Derek Anderson character. Had they put Quinn in and he had turned out to be some sort of wunderkind? Clearly, something was different. There was no time to stop and watch, so I had my brother-in-law whip out his cell phone, which could magically provide live updates from every NFL game. Unfortunately, before he could access this cellular sorcery, we had marched down into the no-signal valley of the subway and were soon hurtling through the dark canyons tunneled beneath the city of Boston.

When we emerged into daylight twenty minutes later, my son was still unconscious and seemed to weigh about seventy-five pounds more than he had back at Fenway. On a shuttle bus, the magic phone came through: the Browns were now up 34–24 midway through the third quarter. Anderson was indeed still in the game and had thrown four touchdown passes. I was stunned. Had he even thrown four touchdown passes in his career? By the time we got back to the car, it was 41–31, and it was time to head to the airport.

My brother-in-law wound up in the other car, so I was without updates for a half hour as we crawled through traffic toward Logan Airport. After dropping off the rental cars (and an unfortunate episode concerning a mysterious dent that had appeared right after we'd relinquished possession), he warmed up his otherworldly cell phone and announced the Browns were up 51–38 with five minutes left. Just like the dent on the front fender of the PT Cruiser, these fifty-one points had come out of absolutely nowhere. I knew then that whatever was going on in Cleveland had historical significance—but also that if the Browns couldn't hang on for the victory, it would be the wrong kind of significance.

The magic cell phone ran out of pixie dust (dead battery) as we waited for yet another shuttle bus, and I once again felt like the Apollo 13 astronauts circling the dark side of the moon. Bouncing on antsy feet like a kid standing outside a soccer field port-a-potty, I crept through the agonizingly slow security check. And as we gathered our dignity from the plastic metal-detector bins, I noticed a bar just across the concourse. On a television screen hanging from the ceiling I saw tiny orange helmets bouncing around. I grabbed my shoes and literally ran in my stocking feet to assess the situation: the Browns were up 51–45 and were punting with a minute to play. "Yeah," I said sarcastically, "there's no way the Browns will let them score." A business traveler beside me didn't catch my cynicism and just started laughing.

Still cradling my shoes like two loaves of bread, I watched nervously as the Bengals picked up two first downs to reach midfield with thirty-three seconds left. Then, the Browns' Leigh Bodden picked off a Carson Palmer pass along the sideline, and I raised my arms in triumph and began jumping up and down in the middle of Logan Airport. Replay held up the call, and the Browns had captured one of the most thrilling victories in recent memory. The glow of triumph got me through an unexplained two-hour flight delay and carried me all the way back home, not unlike how I'd carried my son across Boston earlier that afternoon.

Were it not for the drama the Browns provided, the events of that day would have soon faded into the ordinary continuum of my memory. But because of what was happening in Cleveland, the little details of that sunshiny September afternoon stand out—and strange as it sounds, I know I'll never forget them.

My hope is that you'll experience something similar with the majority of the stories you're about to read. You'll remember not only Dave Logan's touchdown catch or that tackle at the one-yard line that saved the game, but also where you were, whom you were with, and what you were feeling. That's the true beauty of sports—that we become a part of something that serves as a highlighter for life itself, something that brings together strangers and loved ones alike and creates memories that make ordinary days much more vivid than they would otherwise become.

So with the housekeeping out of the way, settle in and let the countdown begin. . . .

#50

BROWNS 15, SAN FRANCISCO 49ERS 12
NOVEMBER 15, 1981

They Found Their Hearts in San Francisco

No one could explain just what had happened to the Kardiac Kids.

In 1980, when the game was on the line (and that was seemingly every week), they could do no wrong on their way to a division title. The following season, the Browns played in just as many close games. But in crunch time in 1981, everything that *could* go wrong *did* go wrong. Up to their hips in expectations, they'd dropped four of their first six games and, after a heart-wrenching overtime loss in Denver in Week Ten, the Browns stood at 4–6—all but mathematically eliminated from a second straight trip to the playoffs.

Still, Browns coach Sam Rutigliano was confident Cleveland could win its final six games and find a way to sneak into the postseason. In fact, Rutigliano said, he expected the streak to start the following Sunday. Needless to say, he was in the minority. The Browns would travel to San Francisco to face the red-hot 49ers, who, after losing thirty-eight of forty-eight games over the previous three seasons, had suddenly become the best team in football. Led by second-year quarterback Joe Montana and a cast of young, relatively unknown players such as wide receiver Dwight Clark and safety Ronnie Lott, the 49ers had won seven straight and entered Week Eleven with a league-best 8–2 mark.

San Francisco was on the brink of a dynasty. On the other hand, the Browns had seen all the excitement and momentum from 1980 evaporate and now just looked like an aging team in need of rebuilding. Naturally, the 49ers weren't exactly quivering at the specter of the deflated Browns coming to town. "We know we're in for one of our toughest games of the year," 49ers coach Bill Walsh groaned sarcastically, taking issue with Rutigliano's prediction.

As the teams traded shots through the media, three days of heavy rain pelted the Bay Area, turning Candlestick Park into a quagmire. By kickoff, the grass was soaked, and the wind wreaked havoc on both teams' passing attacks. The Browns drew first blood when nose tackle Marshall Harris latched onto Montana's legs in the end zone, and the up-and-coming quarterback fired a wayward pass in desperation and was penalized for intentional grounding in the end zone—an automatic safety that gave Cleveland a 2–0 lead.

The Browns' defense hung tough, keeping Montana and Co. from blowing the game open despite a handful of scoring opportunities. Four Ray Wersching field goals gave San Francisco a 12–5 advantage going into the fourth quarter, and it looked like the 49ers were poised to clinch victory when the Browns' Dino Hall lost a fumble on a punt return at his own twenty-one midway through the final period. But after weeks of frustration, the Browns finally came through with a tide-turning play. On the next snap, Cleveland linebacker Dick Ambrose intercepted Montana at the Cleveland six yard line, staving off the backbreaking score. Moments later, Hall redeemed himself with a 40-yard punt return, setting up the game's only touchdown: a 21-yard pass from quarterback Brian Sipe through the stiff wind off the Bay to sliding wideout Reggie Rucker with 6:46 showing to tie the contest.

The Cleveland defense again stood tall, forcing a punt. Then, Sipe and Rucker hooked up again for the play of the day: a 38-yard pass to the 49er twenty-two yard line with 2:29 remaining. It set up a game-winning field-goal attempt by kicker Matt Bahr, who had started the season with San Francisco only to be traded to the Browns after missing four of six kicks as a 49er. Acquired by Cleveland in desperation to replace unreliable David Jacobs after five games, Bahr was perfect on his first game-winning kick in a Browns uniform: a 24-yard boot with forty-three seconds left that gave the Browns a lead they would not relinquish. Cleveland safety Judson Flint clinched the contest moments later by intercepting Montana, securing the biggest upset of the 1981 NFL season.

For one Sunday at least, the Kardiac Kids had returned. And many assumed the victory would be the springboard for a late-season turnaround. Instead, it was the Browns' final win in a disastrous 5–11 campaign. Ironically, it also marked the 49ers' final defeat of 1981—a season that ended with San Francisco winning the first of four Super Bowl titles in the decade.

	1	2	3	4	
Browns	2	3	0	10	=15
49ers	0	6	6	0	=12

First Quarter
   CLE-Safety: Montana penalized for intentional grounding in end zone
Second Quarter
   SF-Wersching 28-yd. FG
   CLE-Bahr 28-yd. FG
   SF-Wersching 29-yd. FG
Third Quarter
   SF-Wersching 28-yd. FG
   SF-Wersching 28-yd. FG
Fourth Quarter
   CLE-Rucker 21-yd. pass from Sipe (Bahr kick)
   CLE-Bahr 24-yd. FG

RUSHING

CLE-M. Pruitt 18–76, G. Pruitt 5–26, White 2–7, Sipe 1–(-3)
SF-Easley 16–59, Hofer 10–33, Patton 4–15, Davis 2–6, Montana 2–5, Solomon 1–0

PASSING

CLE-Sipe 16–33–1–180
SF-Montana 24–42–2–213

RECEIVING

CLE-Rucker 3–77, Newsome 3–36, G. Pruitt 4–33, White 2–12, M. Pruitt 3–11, Feacher 1–11
SF-Hofer 7–64, Clark 6–52, Solomon 3–35, Cooper 3–21, Young 2–16, Patton 1–11, Shuman 1–8, Easley 1–6

BROWNS 28, NEW YORK YANKEES 28
NOVEMBER 23, 1947

Yanking Back the Yankees

Nobody could remember a bigger football weekend in New York City.

On the Sunday before Thanksgiving, three professional games would be played simultaneously within a few miles of one another. At the Polo Grounds, the hometown Giants would face the Green Bay Packers. In Brooklyn's Ebbets Field, the gridiron Dodgers would battle the Los Angeles Dons in the All-American Football Conference, which was gradually gaining both notoriety and acceptance, particularly in the Big Apple.

But the game of the weekend, the game that would draw a larger crowd than the other two combined, was at Yankee Stadium, where the New York football Yankees would host the Cleveland Browns. Not only was it a key matchup between the AAFC's best two teams, but it also appeared it would be a preview of the upcoming league championship, just three weeks away. The 10–1 Browns boasted the best passing offense in the league while the 9–2 Yankees were tops in the AAFC in rushing. The teams had met for the '46 title, and the Browns had won by five, then the Browns took the rematch the following October, extending their win streak over New York to four.

The only other time the Browns had played the Yankees in New York a year earlier, less than 35,000 had filed into Yankee Stadium for a hyped-up Saturday-night affair. This time, 70,060 crammed into the House That Ruth Built on a rainy November Sunday, the largest crowd to attend a football game in New York since Red Grange's professional debut twenty-two years before. The total was more than three times the number that would attend the Packers-Giants NFL contest across town. And the Yankee Stadium fans would get to witness one of the most memorable games in the short-lived history of the All-American Football Conference.

Channeling the frustration of four straight losses to the Browns, the Yanks scored the first four times they had the ball, surging to a seemingly insurmountable 28–0 lead. Behind the power running of Buddy Young and Orban Sanders, who scored the first three touchdowns and rushed for 117 yards in the first half, the heralded New York ground attack was all but unstoppable. Meanwhile, the Browns greased the skids with an early Marion Motley fumble and a pair of interceptions thrown by quarterback Otto Graham. It appeared an AAFC power shift was taking place, and the New York crowd loved every minute of it.

The Browns finally got on the scoreboard before halftime with a 34-yard touchdown pass from Graham to halfback Bill Boedeker, but they still trailed by three touchdowns going into the second half. On their first possession after the break, the Yankees were poised to tack on another touchdown. New York drove to the Cleveland one yard line then sent Cleveland native Eddie Prokop up the middle three straight times, playing the percentages to turn the lights out on the defending champions. But all three times, the beleaguered Browns defense stuffed Prokop, giving the offense back the football. It was the turning point.

On the next play, Graham hit wideout Mac Speedie with a long pass to the Cleveland forty, and Speedie broke free, sprinting to the New York seventeen yard line before being tackled after an 82-yard gain. Two plays after that, Graham connected with Motley for a touchdown to make it 28–14, and the Browns were right back in the game. After the defense forced a punt, Graham and Co. picked up right where they'd left off, driving 80 yards to cut the margin to seven on a 9-yard Motley scoring run.

As the teams battled into the fourth quarter, the Yanks were forced to punt again. This time, the Browns drove ninety yards in fourteen plays and cut the margin to one on a 4-yard touchdown run by Jim Dewar with five minutes left. After Lou Saban—replacing injured Lou Groza as kicker—miraculously sneaked his muffed extra-point kick over the crossbar, the Browns had come all the way back from a twenty-eight-point deficit on the road to tie the game.

But the Yankees had one last drive left in them. They marched to the Cleveland thirty-six yard line, where they faced fourth-and-one with thirty seconds left and the clock running. New York coach Ray Flaherty sent kicker Harvey Johnson in to attempt the game-winning field goal—but forgot to call timeout. Before the Yanks could get the play off, time expired, ending the wildest contest in league history as a fitting 28–28 stalemate.

While New York rolled up 269 yards on the ground, the game's hero was Otto Graham, who passed for an AAFC-record 325 yards on just fifteen completions—an incredible average of better than twenty-one yards per pass.

Even had the Browns lost the game, they still would have won the Western Division title. But would the Browns' 14–3 victory over the Yankees in the AAFC Championship at Yankee Stadium three weeks later have been possible? Or would the reborn Yankees have taken the Browns' place as kingpins of the upstart league?

After that unforgettable Sunday in New York, the Browns would play the talented Yankees five more times before the AAFC disbanded following the 1949 season. Cleveland won all five contests by comfortable margins. In the four-year history of the league, the Browns and Yankees played ten times—and Cleveland never lost.

For the first and only time in the history of sports, a team from Cleveland had a New York team's number. And appropriately, the defining moment of that inexplicable run of domination was also the greatest comeback in franchise history.

	1	2	3	4	
Browns	0	7	14	7	=28
Yankees	14	14	0	0	=28

First Quarter
   NY-Sanders 1-yd. run (Johnson kick)
   NY-Sanders 3-yd. run (Johnson kick)
Second Quarter
   NY-Sanders 27-yd. run (Johnson kick)
   NY-Young 2-yd. run (Johnson kick)
   CLE-Boedeker 34-yd. pass from Graham (Saban kick)
Third Quarter
   CLE-Motley 12-yd. pass from Graham (Saban kick)
   CLE-Motley 9-yd. run (Saban kick)
Fourth Quarter
   CLE-Dewar 4-yd. run (Saban kick)

#48

BROWNS 24, NEW YORK GIANTS 7
DECEMBER 9, 1956

Champs for a Day

After ten years of utter dominance, the Cleveland Browns were suddenly mere mortals. For the first time in their history, they entered the month of December completely out of the title race, and with one more loss, they'd post their first losing season.

As if pouring salt in the wound, in Week Eleven they'd have to travel to Yankee Stadium to face the resurgent New York Giants, who at 7–2–1 were one victory away from clinching their first conference title in a decade. With fifth-year halfback Frank Gifford leading the league in rushing and a coaching staff that included young prodigies Tom Landry and Vince Lombardi, the Giants appeared on the brink of replacing the Browns as the NFL's powerhouse. And nothing would please the Giants or their fans more than beating the rival Browns to complete a season sweep and punch their ticket to the NFL Championship Game.

What's more, the 4–6 Browns would go into the game without starting quarterback George Ratterman or fullback Ed Modzelewski, both out with injury. Not surprisingly, the Giants were eleven-point favorites—the highest point spread the Browns had ever been stacked against. A New York victory seemed automatic, "as inevitable as Santa Claus on Christmas and bowl games on New Year's Day," Chuck Heaton wrote in the *Plain Dealer*. But on a cold, dark day in the Bronx that saw rain showers turn to snow flurries as the afternoon progressed, the Browns simply refused to relinquish their title as defending champions. For one glorious game, the Browns again became the team that had won seven titles over the previous ten seasons—and rained on the Giants' coronation parade.

Perhaps the tone was set at the pre-game meal when the young men the team had selected in the first two rounds of the NFL draft two weeks earlier

9

joined the current players at the Concourse Plaza Hotel: quarterback Milt Plum from Penn State and a slender running back from Syracuse who, Heaton noted, seemed "quietly confident of his ability to make the Browns squad"— Jim Brown.

Things started off well for the visitors when the Giants' Mel Triplett—a University of Toledo product—fumbled an early punt, and Don Paul recovered for the Browns at the New York thirty-four yard line. Five plays later, quarterback Tommy O'Connell—picked up as a free agent in October after Ratterman was injured—marched the Browns through Tom Landry's rugged defense to the New York one yard line, where O'Connell called his own number on third down and lunged across the goal line to give Cleveland a 7–0 lead. After the Giants knotted the contest on a Gifford scoring reception early in the second quarter, the Browns overcame the conditions and a ball covered in sludge and mud to put together a 74-yard drive. They took the lead back with a 41-yard Lou Groza field goal then stretched the margin to ten just before halftime on a short scoring pass from O'Connell to halfback Fred Morrison. Before the Giants could even try to claw back into the contest, the Browns made it 24–7 early in the third quarter when O'Connell again plowed over from the Giant one yard line.

Groza was the catalyst up front, spearheading the offensive line to a dominant performance against the mighty Giants defense. The Browns continually crushed young New York linebacker Sam Huff and rolled up a whopping 193 yards on the ground, including 112 from Morrison. The Cleveland defense was just as dominant, holding Gifford to sixteen yards on six carries and keeping the Giant offense in check throughout the afternoon. Appropriately, New York's only scoring threat of the second half was snuffed out when Paul intercepted Charley Conerly inside the Cleveland ten.

What was left of the small Yankee Stadium crowd spent the fourth quarter mercilessly booing the Giants, who wound up clinching the Eastern crown anyway later that afternoon when the Chicago Cardinals fell to the crosstown-rival Bears. New York went on to clobber the Bears in the NFL Championship two weeks later, bringing a football title to the Big Apple for the first time in eighteen years.

But for one afternoon, the Browns showed their heir apparent they still had a dash of champion left in them.

	1	2	3	4	
Browns	7	10	7	0	=24
Giants	0	7	0	0	=7

First Quarter
CLE-O'Connell 1-yd. run (Groza kick)
Second Quarter
NY-Gifford 6-yd. pass from Conerly (Agajanian kick)
CLE-Groza 41-yd. FG
CLE-Morrison 8-yd. pass from O'Connell (Groza kick)
Third Quarter
CLE-O'Connell 1-yd. run (Groza kick)

RUSHING
CLE-Morrison 19-112, Carpenter 23-70, O'Connell 7-11
NY-Webster 11-46, Triplett 6-41, Gifford 6-16

PASSING
CLE-O'Connell 7-11-1-106
NY-Conerly 10-24-1-103, Clatterbuck 2-3-0-17, Heinrich 2-4-0-6

RECEIVING
CLE-Brewster 3-64, Carpenter 2-28, Morrison 2-14
NY-Gifford 6-56, Rote 1-21, Filipski 2-16, McAfee 1-15, Webster 2-12,
    Chandler 1-5, Triplett 1-1

#47

BROWNS 30, SAN FRANCISCO 49ERS 28
OCTOBER 30, 1949

Football's Greatest Attraction

For almost two full years, the Browns had been untouchable. From October 12, 1947, to October 9, 1949, they didn't lose a game, rattling off a twenty-nine-game unbeaten streak that included back-to-back All-American Football Conference championships.

But just when the Browns were garnering attention and convincing many they were the best team in all of professional football, the San Francisco 49ers spiked their boiler. Cleveland took a 4–0–1 record into Kezar Stadium and got crushed by the upstart 49ers, 56–28. It was the worst loss in Browns history and would stand as the worst loss for another ten years. Not only did it snap the winning streak, it suggested that perhaps San Francisco had leapfrogged the Browns and was now the cream of the AAFC's crop.

As a result, both teams entered their rematch in Cleveland three weeks later with plenty to prove. The winners would proclaim themselves the best in the conference, while the loser would be eliminated from the Western Division race. Fans from across the nation took notice. Better than 72,000 packed into Cleveland Stadium on a crisp autumn afternoon to watch what had quickly become the best rivalry in professional football.

After a scoreless first quarter, the teams exploded for four touchdowns in an eight-minute period. The 49ers drew first blood on a long touchdown pass from Frankie Albert to Len Eshmont, but the Browns responded with an Otto Graham–to–Dante Lavelli score. Before the buzz of the home crowd could diminish, Albert connected with halfback Royal Cathcart for a 72-yard pass that set up another 49er score, but Dub Jones tied matters soon after with a short touchdown run.

The Browns took their first lead early in the third quarter on a 20-yard scoring scamper by Graham. True to form, San Francisco came right back, driving to the Cleveland six yard line. The Browns stopped the 49ers cold and took a 21–14 lead into the fourth quarter, but early in the final stanza, Albert hit Alyn Beals for a 22-yard touchdown that tied the game once again. Of course, the Browns answered, driving into 49er territory and surging ahead with 9:45 remaining on Lou Groza's first field goal of the season. The Cleveland defense then came up with a huge stop that gave the offense a chance to put the game away. And that's precisely what happened: Graham hit Mac Speedie for the clinching touchdown on a clutch fourth-down pass with five minutes left to make it 30–21. The 49ers added another touchdown with fifteen seconds left, but it was too little, too late. The Browns had reasserted themselves as the league's best in the most thrilling game in their young history.

The teams had combined for fifty-eight points and nearly 900 yards of offense, more than 500 of which came through the air—using a new brand of football that would soon revolutionize the game. What's more, the Browns-49ers rivalry had superseded the minor-league reputation of the All-American Conference. More than a half-million fans had attended the eight games the teams had now played against one another. They'd saved their best for last. "This was another fitting addition to the Cleveland-San Francisco series that now ranks as the greatest attraction in professional football," Harold Sauerbrei wrote in the *Plain Dealer*.

"It was a tough, dogged fight and my hat's off to you," Paul Brown told his players afterward. "I've had this game inside me for two weeks. Believe me, I was worried, but you did a great job."

And this game—along with both squads' spectacular seasons—further paved the way for both the Browns and 49ers to successfully make the leap to the NFL the following season.

	1	2	3	4	
49ers	0	14	0	14	=28
Browns	0	14	7	9	=30

Second Quarter
    SF-Eshmont 48-yd. pass from Albert (Vetrano kick)
    CLE-Lavelli 9-yd. pass from Graham (Groza kick)
    SF-Lillywhite 8-yd. run (Vetrano kick)
    CLE-Jones 6-yd. run (Groza kick)

Third Quarter
    CLE-Graham 20-yd. run (Groza kick)
Fourth Quarter
    SF-Beals 22-yd. pass from Albert (Vetrano kick)
    CLE-Groza 38-yd. FG
    CLE-Speedie 11-yd. pass from Graham (kick failed)
    SF-Albert 1-yd. run (Vetrano kick)

RUSHING
SF-Cathcart 11–116, Albert 5–57, Perry 10–27, Lillywhite 7–20, Standlee
    2–2, Beals 1–2
CLE-Graham 8–43, Motley 9–34, Jones 13–33, Boedeker 4–16, Adamle 1–3,
    James 1–0

PASSING
SF-Albert 14–27–0–253
CLE-Graham 14–25–0–271

RECEIVING
SF-Cathcart 5–88, Beals 4–78, Eshmont 1–48, Shoener 2–24, Solata 1–14,
    Lillywhite 1–1
CLE-Speedie 6–99, Lavelli 3–73, Motley 3–55, Gillom 1–29, Boedeker 1–15

BROWNS 24, ATLANTA FALCONS 16
DECEMBER 29, 2002

Run, William, Run!

It had been eight years since the Browns were in this position—but to the fans it seemed like 800.

Much had changed since the last time their football team qualified for the NFL playoffs, not the least of which was the original franchise moving from Cleveland. But if the cards fell correctly the Sunday after Christmas, the Browns would be heading for the postseason for the first time since 1994.

But even if all the scenarios aligned, they would be meaningless if the Browns couldn't defeat the visiting Atlanta Falcons, who themselves were fighting for a playoff berth. With a last-minute victory in Baltimore the previous Sunday, the Browns had ensured their first non-losing season since their return, but appropriately after the way the preposterous 2002 campaign had unfolded, their fate would be determined at the last possible moment. The final act would play out at Cleveland Browns Stadium, where the team was just 2–5 on the year while a robust 6–2 on the road.

From the "Helmet-Gate" debacle in Week One in which the Browns lost after time had expired when linebacker Dwayne Rudd was penalized for throwing his helmet in celebration, to the bizarre Hail Mary victory in Jacksonville in Week Fourteen, the '02 Browns lived and died in the game's final moments. Ten of their fifteen games had been decided in the last minute. "It's unbelievable," said quarterback Tim Couch, who had endured a painfully awkward season during which the offense seemed to function better under backup Kelly Holcomb. "We're still in the thick of things."

Considering the team was just a year removed from a hellish 3–13 season, simply to have a shot to qualify for the playoffs in Week Seventeen seemed like a minor miracle. "The guys that have been around here are looking forward to this situation," said cornerback Daylon McCutcheon, one of the few remaining players who had suffered through the 2–14 expansion campaign of 1999. "This is what we've been dreaming about."

As had the fans, who packed into Cleveland Browns Stadium and brought the crystal palace on the shores of Lake Erie to life for the first time all season. The Browns surged to an early lead, then the herky-jerky season took another incredible turn. On the first play of the second quarter, Couch broke his right leg and was replaced by Holcomb, who hadn't taken a snap since Week Five when he'd suffered a hairline fracture on his foot in a heartbreaking loss to the Ravens. As Holcomb tried to shake off the rust, the Falcons clawed back from a 10–0 deficit and took a 16–10 lead with a trio of third-quarter field goals aided by a pair of Cleveland turnovers.

But as they had all year, the Browns hung close and got the break they needed when defensive lineman Gerard Warren recovered an Atlanta fumble at the Falcon eleven yard line midway through the fourth quarter. Holcomb finally found the end zone two plays later when he connected with wideout Kevin Johnson—another holdover from the '99 team—for a 15-yard touchdown pass on third-and-fourteen with 6:58 remaining. The Browns led 17–16 but weren't out of the woods yet.

After forcing an Atlanta punt, the Browns took over at their own twenty-nine with less than five minutes to play, stuck between trying to melt the clock and pulling out the stops for an insurance touchdown. That's when William Green provided the play of the year.

The rookie running back from Boston College, who had caught fire in the second half of the season, took a handoff on a typical off-tackle play on second-and-three at the Cleveland thirty-six, stutter-stepped, then broke through the line. He stumbled, broke a tackle, and then sprinted down the sideline, with the roar of the Stadium crowd swelling with each step. Up in the radio booth, Browns play-by-play announcer Jim Donovan interrupted his description of the play to become a fan for one unforgettable moment, crying, *"Run, William, run!"*

After what seemed like an eternity, Green finally reached the end zone, and the capacity crowd exploded. The Browns now led 24–16 with 3:53 remaining. But even after the heroics of Green, who had rushed for 178 yards on the day, they weren't in the clear.

Guided by phenom rookie quarterback Michael Vick, Atlanta drove to the Cleveland four yard line with 1:23 left and was poised to tie the contest and send the Browns to overtime for the third time in 2002. Running back Warrick Dunn crashed forward for three yards to the Cleveland one on first-and-goal, then Dwayne Rudd stepped up to exorcize a phantom that had haunted him for sixteen weeks. He blanketed tight end Alge Crumpler on second down, forcing Vick to throw the ball away. Third down was another handoff to Dunn, and Rudd crushed him for no gain. With the clock ticking down under thirty seconds and the Stadium in an uproar, the entire season would boil down to one play. *"This is typical Browns stuff for you,"* Donovan told his audience. *"Nothing but plenty of drama."*

Vick took the snap and again handed off to Dunn up the middle. And this time, linebacker Earl Holmes crashed through the line to stop Dunn dead in his tracks short of the goal line. The Browns defense sprinted victoriously off the field as the hometown crowd flooded the team in a tidal wave of emotion. "All those close games were for today," jubilant Cleveland coach Butch Davis told his team in the locker room afterward, "to know how to handle the pressure with composure, to know how to trust each other late in the game." As dramatically as he'd blown the opener, Rudd had saved the finale, pulling himself off the hook in the process. "It gives me a chance to get a little more sleep at night," a relieved Rudd said. "It's over. Life goes on."

The party was on in downtown Cleveland, capped three hours later as the final seconds ticked down in a blowout victory by the New York Jets over the Green Bay Packers—the final piece to the Browns' playoff puzzle. "We're all living our dream right now," Green said.

And for the fans, who had waited eight long years, it was also the end of a nightmare.

	1	2	3	4	
Falcons	0	7	9	0	=16
Browns	3	7	0	14	=24

First Quarter
CLE-Dawson 40-yd. FG
Second Quarter
CLE-Green 21-yd. run (Dawson kick)
ATL-Finneran 15-yd. pass from Vick (Feely kick)
Third Quarter
ATL-Feely 42-yd. FG
ATL-Feely 49-yd. FG
ATL-Feely 30-yd. FG
Fourth Quarter
CLE-Johnson 15-yd. pass from Holcomb (Dawson kick)
CLE-Green 64-yd. run (Dawson kick)

RUSHING

ATL-Dunn 20–67, Vick 6–37, Duckett 1–0

CLE-Green 27–178, Northcutt 2–10, White 1–2, Holcomb 4–(-1)

PASSING

ATL-Vick 17–40–1–240

CLE-Holcomb 7–14–2–86, Couch 7–11–1–68

RECEIVING

ATL-Finneran 3–77, McCord 3–65, Crumpler 2–34, Gaylor 3–30, Dunn 3–14, Layne 2–11, Kelly 1–9

CLE-Davis 2–36, Johnson 3–32, Morgan 2–32, Northcutt 1–22, Campbell 1–12, Heiden 2–9, Green 2–9, White 1–2

#45

BROWNS 14, NEW YORK GIANTS 13
OCTOBER 28, 1951

Puncturing the Umbrella

The New York Giants had been waiting ten long months for this game.

Neither the Giants nor their fans had forgotten the historic American Conference playoff the previous December, in which the Browns pulled off a narrow victory over New York on the frozen Cleveland Stadium turf. The Giants had defeated Cleveland twice in the regular season, and, some felt, New York had outplayed the Browns a third time in the playoff. But the Browns prevailed and won the right to play in the 1950 NFL Championship Game.

Nothing reflected the Giants' effort better than the way their defense smothered the high-octane Cleveland offense. In their three encounters in 1950, the Browns had scored just one touchdown, and that was after recovering a fumble at the Giant one yard line. The Giants were the only team that had consistently frustrated the Browns in their wildly successful six-year history. The secret was New York's quirky "umbrella" defense that stacked the defensive backfield and dropped two linemen into coverage along the sidelines.

Now, nearly a year later, the teams would meet again at Cleveland Stadium, this time with first place in the conference on the line. At 3–0–1, the Giants were the NFL's only undefeated team and also brought the league's top-ranked defense to this encounter for the inside track to the '51 title. "This is the game the Browns must win or all but write off their hopes of keeping the National League championship," Harold Sauerbrei wrote in the *Plain Dealer*. "But, to do it they must be able to score some points."

Yet after failing to drive to the end zone against the Giants in 180 minutes of play in 1950, it took the Browns a mere forty-nine seconds in 1951. On the first play of the game, Otto Graham hit a streaking Dub Jones for a 64-yard touchdown pass that delighted the home crowd of 56,000-plus—the NFL's largest crowd of the weekend. It was an auspicious start for Graham, who would puncture the Giants' "umbrella" for twelve completions in seventeen attempts in the first thirty minutes. But a pair of those five incompletions changed the complexion of the game. First, after the Browns recovered a Giant fumble at the New York twenty-eight yard line moments after Jones's touchdown, Graham was picked off in the end zone. Shortly after, Cleveland's Emerson Cole couldn't hang on to a pass, and it bounced into the arms of Giants defensive back Tom Landry at the Cleveland twenty. Landry raced into the end zone to tie the game at seven.

But the Browns responded after recovering another Giant fumble with a 26-yard Graham–to–Dante Lavelli third-down scoring pass that gave them back the lead. It appeared the three defensive struggles of 1950 would yield to an offensive fireworks show, particularly when the Giants scored again to make it 14–13 five minutes into the second quarter. Ray Poole missed the extra point, however, and the Browns clung to a one-point lead. Suddenly, the game reverted back to the type of defensive slobberknocker the teams had waged three times the year before.

To counter the red-hot Graham, the Giants modified their "umbrella," adding yet another defensive back to the mixture. Also having to combat a strengthening wind rising up off Lake Erie, the Browns quarterback cooled, and Cleveland never threatened to score in the second half, though they hurt their own cause with 115 yards in penalties. Meanwhile, the Cleveland defense—led by lineman Bill Willis—rose to the occasion, stymieing Giant running back Eddie Price, the NFL's leading rusher. Price could manage just sixty-one yards on twenty-four carries on the day, and New York only crossed midfield twice without the aid of penalties—on that second occasion, it appeared they were poised to steal victory from the Browns' grasp.

With less than three minutes remaining, New York took over at its own thirty-eight yard line and drove to the Cleveland thirty-three. With a minute to play, Poole was called on to atone for his earlier missed extra point to try to win the game with a 40-yard field goal. Poole had enough distance, and for much of the kick, the trajectory was true. But at the last moment, an October breeze rushed in off the lake and pushed the football wide just before it passed through the uprights.

The Browns ran out the clock and vaulted over the Giants into first place. There they would remain, with the critical victory over New York serving as the fourth of what would become an eleven-game winning streak that propelled Cleveland back to the NFL title game.

	1	2	3	4	
Giants	7	6	0	0	=13
Browns	14	0	0	0	=14

First Quarter
  CLE-Jones 64-yd. pass from Graham (Groza kick)
  NY-Landry 20-yd. INT return (Poole kick)
  CLE-Lavelli 26-yd. pass from Graham (Groza kick)
Second Quarter
  NY-McChesney 29-yd. pass from Conerly (kick failed)

RUSHING
NY-Price 24–61, Scott 12–52, Conerly 1–(-1), Tidwell 1–(-2)
CLE-Graham 8–26, Groza 1–16, Cole 5–12, Bumgardner 13–7, Motley 1–4,
    Jones 6–0

PASSING
NY-Conerly 9–13–1–117, Tidwell 0–1–1–0
CLE-Graham 16–24–3–216

RECEIVING
NY-Scott 3–48, McChesney 1–29, Stribling 3–24, Price 1–4, Sulaitis 1–2
CLE-Jones 7–116, Lavelli 6–68, Gillom 2–25, Bumgardner 1–7

the Browns responded when Leroy Kelly swept around left end and found the end zone from three yards out to make it 7–3 at the half. Another O'Brien field goal in the third quarter cut the margin to one going into the fourth quarter of what had become a defensive slugfest.

The Cleveland defense gradually took control of the game, racking up five interceptions and two fumble recoveries while holding the Colts to 178 yards of total offense and just three completed passes. So when Kelly added a second touchdown to put the Browns up 14–6 with twelve minutes left, it appeared Cleveland was coasting to an upset victory.

But with 4:25 remaining, Baltimore linebacker Ted Hendricks blocked a Don Cockroft punt, and the Colts' Don Nottingham—a Kent State graduate—returned it twenty yards for a touchdown to pull the home team within a point. The crowd of 56,000-plus was suddenly roaring after an afternoon of subdued silence.

The Baltimore backers got even more excited when the home team got the ball back with just over two minutes left and drove to midfield. Facing fourth down with the game on the line, Johnny Unitas—in for an ineffective Earl Morrall—threw long. Browns rookie cornerback Clarence Scott then made the mistake of intercepting the pass deep in his own territory rather than knocking it down and taking possession at the fifty yard line. Scott was tackled at the Browns six, and with the Browns' lead just one point, the game was still far from over.

With thirty seconds left, the Browns were forced to punt from inside their five yard line. Cockroft, who'd already had one punt blocked for a touchdown, another partially blocked, and missed a pair of field goals, was not having a good day. Another mistake here could cost the Browns the game. However, this time, not only did Cockroft get the kick off, he launched a bomb that soared well out of range for O'Brien to win the game. The ball then hit the soft turf and rolled all the way back to the Baltimore thirty-three with twenty-one seconds to play. The Browns added even more superfluous drama on the game's final play when Walt Sumner picked off a Unitas pass deep in Cleveland territory, only to attempt a lateral that the Colts recovered as time expired.

Despite the overall sloppiness of the contest, the Browns had prevailed, winning their seventh straight game in Baltimore and setting the tone for a turnaround season that ended with their first-ever AFC Central Division title. Perhaps even more importantly, for one rainy September Sunday the Browns had proven to be even more super than the defending world champions—and in the process, reminded their fans how wonderful a victory in a big game could feel.

"There sure must be a lot of happy people back in Cleveland tonight," said Shaw High School product Tom Matte in the sullen Baltimore locker room. "They really love those Browns, don't they?"

	1	2	3	4	
Browns	0	7	0	7	=14
Colts	0	3	3	7	=13

Second Quarter
BAL-O'Brien 27-yd. FG
CLE-Kelly 3-yd. run (Cockroft kick)
Third Quarter
BAL-O'Brien 32-yd. FG
Fourth Quarter
CLE-Kelly 1-yd. run (Cockroft kick)
BAL-Nottingham 20-yd. return of blocked punt (O'Brien kick)

RUSHING
CLE-Scott 19–68, Kelly 19–56, Nelsen 1–(-1), Morrison 1–(-5)
BAL-Bulaich 11–63, Matte 11–41, Nottingham 8–40, Morrall 1–7

PASSING
CLE-Nelsen 13–26–2–161
BAL-Morrall 3–13–3–49, Unitas 0–5–2–0

RECEIVING
CLE-Hooker 6–78, Collins 3–58, Scott 3–17, Morin 1–8
BAL-Matte 1–22, Mackey 1–16, Perkins 1–11

#43

MIAMI DOLPHINS 24, BROWNS 21
JANUARY 4, 1986

Crashing the Party

The Browns had become the first team in NFL history to make the playoffs and yet be criticized for doing so.

It had been a strange season in 1985. The Browns showed remarkable improvement after a disastrous 5–11 finish the year before and appeared to be only a year or two away from becoming one of the elite teams in the AFC, posting a respectable 8–8 record. Bizarrely, their .500 tally was good enough to win the mediocre Central Division and earn an invitation to the playoffs, while more deserving squads such as the 11–5 Denver Broncos and 10–6 Washington Redskins failed to qualify.

Not surprisingly, the Browns became the butt of jokes in the national media, which all but called for a court order to keep Cleveland from the playoffs. Perhaps all that prevented it was the Browns' "reward" for backing into the postseason: they would face the mighty Miami Dolphins, the defending AFC champions. Led by dazzling young quarterback Dan Marino and heralded wide receivers Mark Duper and Mark Clayton, Miami boasted the best offense in football and seemed a sure bet to return to the Super Bowl. Though the Browns defense had shown flashes of brilliance the past two seasons under new coach Marty Schottenheimer, seemingly everyone agreed the Dolphins, 10½-point favorites, would cruise past these party-crashers in their divisional playoff in the Orange Bowl, where Miami had won eleven straight.

Instead, in the first half, it was the Browns who looked dominant. The defense consistently confused Marino as cornerbacks Hanford Dixon and Frank Minnifield completely shut down Duper and Clayton. "By the second half, Marino didn't even bother to look their way," Minnifield said. "He knew we had taken away their home-run hitters." Meanwhile, the Cleveland offense employed a high school game plan that utilized running backs Kevin Mack and Earnest Byner—each of whom had rushed for 1,000 yards in the regular season—and a ball-control philosophy. Early on, it worked like a charm.

The Browns capped a long drive with a touchdown pass from rookie Bernie Kosar to tight end Ozzie Newsome that gave them a 7–3 lead. Miami was poised to surge back ahead, driving to the Browns seven yard line, but Cleveland safety Don Rogers picked off Marino at the goal line and returned the football to midfield. It set up an incredible 21-yard touchdown run by Byner in which he eluded five would-be tacklers on his way to the end zone. The double-digit underdogs now *led* by double digits at the half, and football fans from coast to coast were stunned.

Things got even stranger early in the third quarter when Byner—playing the game of his life—broke free for a 66-yard touchdown run on a trap play that gave the Browns a 21–3 lead. *"Boy, that was shades of Leroy Kelly, Jim Brown and a few others,"* an impressed Nev Chandler told his radio audience. The upstart Cleveland Browns, who most football fans determined didn't even belong in the playoffs, were now twenty-four minutes away from one of the biggest upsets in NFL history. But the Dolphins wouldn't cooperate with the script.

Marino directed two quick scoring drives to cut the margin to four heading into the fourth period. Though the momentum had clearly swung, the Browns hung tough, forcing a Miami punt midway through the fourth and giving the offense a chance to kill the clock. On a critical third-and-two at the Miami forty-eight yard line with eight minutes remaining, Byner misheard the call in the huddle and didn't lead the blocking on a pitch to Curtis Dickey, who was crushed for a six-yard loss. It was the only down moment of the day for Byner, who would rush for 161 yards on sixteen carries—setting a Browns playoff record. "I showed a lot of people around the nation what type of running back Earnest Byner really is," Byner said.

The Browns were forced to punt, and the Dolphins caught fire once again. Marino hit tailback Tony Nathan for a spirit-breaking 38-yard pass, and Miami reached the Cleveland one at the two-minute warning. Ron Davenport scored on the next play to put the Dolphins ahead, and the Browns' run-oriented offense was unable to cross midfield on its final, harried drive.

The Browns and their fans were crushed, but they still had plenty to be proud of. They'd silenced their numerous critics by pressing one of the NFL's best teams to the wall. "We showed people throughout the country we do have a ball club, and we deserved to be in the playoffs," Minnifield said.

An up-and-down 1985 season had ended on an inspiring note, and the tone had been set for a run of brilliance the city of Cleveland had waited two decades to see.

	1	2	3	4	
Browns	7	7	7	0	=21
Dolphins	3	0	14	7	=24

First Quarter
MIA-Reveiz 51-yd. FG
CLE-Newsome 16-yd. pass from Kosar (Bahr kick)
Second Quarter
CLE-Byner 21-yd. run (Bahr kick)
Third Quarter
CLE-Byner 66-yd. run (Bahr kick)
MIA-Moore 6-yd. pass from Marino (Reveiz kick)
MIA-Davenport 31-yd. run (Reveiz kick)
Fourth Quarter
MIA-Davenport 1-yd. run (Reveiz kick)

RUSHING
CLE-Byner 16–161, Mack 13–56, Dickey 6–28, Kosar 2–6
MIA-Davenport 6–48, Nathan 7–21, Bennett 8–17, Paige 2–6

PASSING
CLE-Kosar 10–19–1–66
MIA-Marino 25–45–1–238

RECEIVING
CLE-Byner 4–25, Newsome 2–22, Weathers 1–12, Fontenot 1–5, Holt 2–2
MIA-Nathan 10–101, Hardy 5–51, Moore 4–29, Rose 1–17, Clayton 1–15, Johnson 2–17, Bennett 1–6, Carter 1–2

#42

BROWNS 31, SAN FRANCISCO 49ERS 28
NOVEMBER 28, 1948

Something Like Awe

The unforgettable 1948 presidential election that saw Harry Truman score an upset victory over Thomas Dewey three weeks earlier was still fresh in the minds of the American public. But in the course of their respective campaigns, neither Truman nor Dewey had embarked on a road trip quite as ambitious as the one the Browns began Thanksgiving week.

They would travel 7,000 miles and play three critical games in just eight days without returning to Cleveland. After a victory over the Yankees in New York, the Browns flew all night to Los Angeles, where they would face the Dons on Thanksgiving morning three days later. From there it was on to San Francisco for the game of the year—a battle with the 49ers for the AAFC West Division title.

In case there wasn't already enough pressure as the Browns embarked on their cross-country gauntlet, the win in New York was the team's fourteenth straight, and the Browns were now just two wins away from becoming the third professional team to post a perfect season. "Without question, the Browns are the greatest team in professional football," Dons coach Jim Phelan said that week. "They probably are the greatest team ever assembled."

The Browns looked the part on Thanksgiving, overcoming fatigue to score seventeen unanswered points in the second half to defeat the Dons 31–14 at the Los Angeles Coliseum before 60,000 fans. The win was their fifteenth straight. Their reward was a two-hour plane ride to Oakland, followed by a two-hour bus trip to remote Boyes Springs, where the team would get a mere two days to prepare for the game of the year. "Thus," wrote Harold Sauerbrei in the *Plain Dealer*, "the Browns' chances of defeating the powerful 49ers for the second time this season appear dim."

And when Paul Brown missed an interview session to hurriedly prepare for the 11–1 49ers, the Bay Area newspapers turned on him. Reporters began to question the Browns' lofty reputation, claiming the only reason they'd been so successful was because they'd been permitted to get away with illegal blocking maneuvers. As if rubbing salt in the wound, Otto Graham had dinged his knee in the Los Angeles game and was limping badly throughout practice on Friday. While some pressured Brown to throw caution to the wind and start Graham, the coach was wary. "We may use him today and ruin him for the rest of the year," Brown said. "It's entirely up to him." But it appeared as though it would be up to backup Cliff Lewis, a Lakewood native, to guide the Browns to their third straight division title.

Conversely, not only did the 49ers get the entire week off to prepare for the Browns, they were the hottest offensive team in football. In a mind-boggling 63–40 win over the Brooklyn Dodgers the prior Sunday, the teams had combined to break sixteen records. Along the way, the 49ers became the first team to score sixty touchdowns in a season. While the Browns offense was strong, averaging twenty-seven points per contest, San Francisco was even better—averaging nearly thirty-six. The Browns defense had dominated the 49ers in a 14–7 victory in Cleveland two weeks earlier, but considering the week the Browns had endured, a repeat performance seemed unlikely. For the first time in their history, the Browns were underdogs.

In front of the largest crowd to ever attend a game in San Francisco, Cleveland received two unexpected sparks right after kickoff. The 49ers fumbled on the first play, and Tony Adamle recovered for the Browns at the 49er forty-one yard line. Then Graham decided to put himself in the game and limped onto the field. On his first play, the hobbling quarterback hit Dante Lavelli for a touchdown and a 7–0 Browns lead. The advantage swelled to ten on a Lou Groza field goal following another fumble, but then the 49ers caught fire.

The capacity crowd at Kezar Stadium watched in delight as San Francisco surged to a 14–10 halftime lead, then expanded it to 21–10 early in the third quarter. Moments later, Graham fumbled, and the 49ers recovered in Cleveland territory. The Browns were battered and tired, and the 49ers were poised to land the knockout punch.

But the Cleveland defense—which had struggled for much of the contest—rose to the occasion, stopping San Francisco on downs at the Cleveland twenty-seven yard line and giving the ball back to the offense. In the next eight minutes, Graham put on a show, tossing three more touchdown passes to give the Browns a 31–21 lead. The once-rambunctious Kezar crowd was hushed. "Under the circumstances," Brown said later, "it was Otto's greatest performance." Even the antagonistic San Francisco media was forced to agree. "I think we'll honor Graham as the best in football," one veteran West Coast reporter noted in the press box.

San Francisco wouldn't quit, driving seventy-nine yards to narrow the lead to three with seven minutes to play on Frankie Albert's third touchdown pass. With fatigue at its peak, the Browns responded like champions, controlling the ball for the next six minutes on a methodical drive to the San Francisco twelve. By the time the 49ers regained possession, a mere fifty seconds remained, and they couldn't reach midfield before time expired, giving the Browns the most improbable victory in their young history. "Determination, skill, courage when the odds were stacked heavily against them," Sauerbrei wrote, "Cleveland's stalwart Browns had all these today."

The exhausted Browns had won their sixteenth straight game, kept their chances for a perfect season alive, held off a well-rested rival following a nightmarish road trip, and most importantly, secured a trip to the AAFC championship game. Wrote Gordon Cobbledick in the *Plain Dealer:* "The grandstand bugs and the professional critics alike are beginning to speak of the Browns with something like awe."

	1	2	3	4	
Browns	10	0	21	0	=31
49ers	0	14	7	7	=28

First Quarter
    CLE-Lavelli 41-yd. pass from Graham (Groza kick)
    CLE-Groza 21-yd. FG
Second Quarter
    SF-Perry 3-yd. run (Vetrano kick)
    SF-Beals 4-yd. pass from Albert (Vetrano kick)
Third Quarter
    SF-Beals 29-yd. pass from Albert (Vetrano kick)
    CLE-Motley 6-yd. pass from Graham (Groza kick)
    CLE-D. Jones 20-yd. pass from Graham (Groza kick)
    CLE-E. Jones 33-yd. pass from Graham (Groza kick)
Fourth Quarter
    SF-Perry 14-yd. pass from Albert (Vetrano kick)

#41

Meet Brian Sipe

Nick Skorich had seen enough.

The fourth-year coach had seen his Browns wobble to their worst start ever, losing five of their first six games, and they were now riding a franchise-record four-game losing streak. He knew if they didn't turn things around quickly, he might not survive the season as coach.

So when quarterback Mike Phipps—who'd been disappointing all year—threw yet another interception on the first play of the fourth quarter with the Browns trailing by twelve, Skorich took action. With much of the Cleveland Stadium crowd already heading for the exits, he benched the ineffective Phipps for a backup whose only other NFL appearance had resulted in two complete passes and three interceptions. In that moment, Browns history was changed forever.

"OK, all you hero-starved Cleveland Browns fans," Chuck Heaton would write in the *Plain Dealer* the next day, "we've finally found one for you . . . He's got the hands of a brain surgeon, the heart of a lion, legs like Nureyev, and he's better-looking than Robert Redford. He's the U.S. Cavalry to the rescue . . . He's tougher than Kojak and smarter than Kissinger . . .

"Meet Brian Sipe."

As the October sun glided toward the horizon that warm autumn afternoon, Cleveland fans were introduced to this man named Sipe. Prior to this day, they knew little about him. He was a thirteenth-round draft choice from pass-happy San Diego State two years earlier, but he could only land a spot on the practice squad until 1974. No one gave any thought to the notion of Sipe as a starter because, for better or worse, Mike Phipps was the signal-caller of the future. But with the bottom about to drop out on the season, the future was now. And it was up to Sipe to save the day.

After a clever 27-yard pass from Don Cockroft to Van Green on a fake punt on fourth-and-twelve seemed to awaken the slumbering Browns, Sipe connected on the first clutch pass of his career. On fourth-and-ten moments later, Sipe improvised on a broken play and hit wideout Steve Holden for thirteen yards and a first down. Then Sipe finished the drive with an eight-yard touchdown scramble that pulled the Browns within five.

And when the Browns defense forced a Denver punt minutes later, another future Browns legend made his dramatic debut. Second-year running back Greg Pruitt, used sparingly in 1973, was just starting to find his niche, slowly becoming an integral part of the Browns offense and special teams. Battling the autumn sun, it took all of Pruitt's concentration simply to catch the lofty punt, but then the small but elusive scatback from Oklahoma carved through the Bronco defense downfield, not stopping until he was tripped up at the Denver three yard line following a 72-yard return.

It set up the winning touchdown moments later, scored, appropriately, by Sipe. From the Denver one, Sipe tried to plow through the line but hit a wall of humanity and floundered backward. "I bounced off and was still standing," Sipe said. "It gave me another chance." Sipe spun around and flung himself into the end zone with 1:56 remaining to give the Browns their first lead. When a long Denver field goal fell short in the final seconds, Sipe completed the first comeback of his career. Fans scampered onto the field and mobbed him on his way back to the locker room.

"It was the team's performance that did it today," Sipe said modestly. "I just went about my business, and they went about theirs." But Sipe's instant success seemed to have little to do with the technical aspects of his game. Heaton noted—not for the last time—that "the luck of the team seemed to turn from bad to good with the Californian at the controls."

Though the bulk of their success was still a few years away, the heroics of Sipe and Pruitt proved that golden afternoon would go down in history as the day the Kardiac Kids were born.

	1	2	3	4	
Denver	7	7	7	0	=21
Cleveland	0	3	6	14	=23

First Quarter
DEN-Odoms 12-yd. pass from Johnson (Turner kick)

Second Quarter
  CLE-Cockroft 27-yd. FG
  DEN-Simmons 13-yd. pass from Johnson (Turner kick)
Third Quarter
  CLE-Cockroft 30-yd. FG
  CLE-Cockroft 25-yd. FG
  DEN-Armstrong 33-yd. run (Turner kick)
Fourth Quarter
  CLE-Sipe 8-yd. run (Cockroft kick)
  CLE-Sipe 1-yd. run (Cockroft kick)

RUSHING
DEN-Armstrong 17–142, Little 13–41, Keyworth 1–2, Ross 1–1
CLE-McKinnis 7–23, Pruitt 7–22, Brown 7–15

PASSING
DEN-Johnson 14–24–1–207
CLE-Phipps 8–25–1–170, Sipe 4–6–0–32, Cockroft 1–1–0–27

RECEIVING
DEN-Odoms 4–59, Little 4–37, Simmons 2–34, Thaxton 1–34, Armstrong
  2–23, Moses 1–17
CLE-McKinnis 6–111, Van Heusen 1–37, Richardson 2–32, Van Green 1–27,
  Holden 2–21, Pruitt 1–4

Bengals—who had throttled the Browns 30–0 in their last meeting—Quinn would make his NFL debut.

Thus, the stage was set for a historic afternoon at Cleveland Browns Stadium simply because almost every soul in the ballpark anticipated seeing Quinn, certainly not a Cleveland victory. Things started true to form when the red-hot Bengals offense scored a touchdown on its first possession, and Anderson misfired on his first five pass attempts. The Quinn countdown was on. But after the Browns intercepted Cincy quarterback Carson Palmer to set up a field goal, Anderson showed signs of life, driving his team fifty-nine yards for another field goal to cut the lead to one going into a second quarter that would be un-like any other quarter in Cleveland history.

Anderson threw three touchdown passes in the next fifteen minutes as the contest turned into a pinball-machine offensive slugfest. When the Browns surged ahead 13–7, Palmer and Co. went right back up by one, then Cleveland kick returner Josh Cribbs returned the ensuing kickoff eighty-five yards to set up Anderson's second scoring pass in five minutes to veteran wideout Joe Jurevicius to make it 20–14. Palmer answered with an 88-yard drive, capped by a 22-yard touchdown toss to flamboyant wide receiver Chad Johnson—who the previous week had brazenly pledged to leap into the Dog Pound bleach-ers if he scored a touchdown at that end of the field. Anderson continued his improbable performance with a 25-yard touchdown pass to tight end Kellen Winslow, Jr. to put the Browns up six at the half.

The lead swelled to ten on the Browns' first possession of the third quarter when Anderson capped a 78-yard march with a 34-yard touchdown pass to wideout Braylon Edwards. Naturally, Palmer countered with another score to Johnson, and as promised, the Bengals wideout leapt into the Pound, where he was showered by beer and food tossed from the fired-up Browns faithful. The fireworks continued. On the next snap, running back Jamal Lewis, signed by the Browns in the off-season to shore up their oft-invisible running game, snapped through the line of scrimmage for a 66-yard touchdown run to make it 41–31 with six minutes still to play in the third quarter. The Bengals then cut the margin back to three with Palmer's fifth touchdown pass just before the start of the fourth quarter.

Once again, Anderson defied expectation, driving the Browns 92 yards in five plays and putting them back up by two scores with a 37-yard scoring toss to Edwards. The wiry quarterback who'd had five touchdown passes in his career going into the season had now matched that total in one afternoon. Back-to-back stops by the Cleveland defense set up another field goal, and the home team took a 51–38 lead into the final five minutes. Palmer parlayed his hot hand into another touchdown—his sixth scoring toss of the game—to cut it to 51–45 with 3:39 left. After the Browns were forced to punt with just over a minute to play, Palmer and the Cincinnati offense would have a chance to thwart all of Anderson's incredible achievements.

From their own eight yard line, the Bengals quickly reached midfield, then Palmer's fiftieth pass of the afternoon was intercepted along the sideline by Browns cornerback Leigh Bodden with twenty seconds remaining. Appropriately, Anderson, who had been at the center of a tempest of ridicule for the entire franchise, took a knee on the final snap of perhaps the most improbable victory in franchise history.

It was the highest-scoring football game ever played in Cleveland. The teams combined for twelve touchdowns, fifty-six first downs, ninety-six points, and 1,085 total yards. After their initial three-and-out, the Browns went on to score on nine of their next thirteen possessions behind newfound hero Anderson, who tossed for a career-best 328 yards. Edwards and Winslow each tallied 100 receiving yards, while Lewis exploded for 215 on the ground—the Browns' first 200-yard rushing game in thirty-two years. And at the center of this electric display of offense was an unproven youngster from Scappoose, Oregon.

"I had a lot of fun out there today," Anderson said quaintly afterward.

Following a week of unprecedented embarrassment, so did the Browns.

	1	2	3	4	
Bengals	7	14	17	7	=45
Browns	6	21	14	10	=51

First Quarter
    CIN-R. Johnson 13-yd. pass from Palmer (Graham kick)
    CLE-Dawson 39-yd. FG
    CLE-Dawson 39-yd. FG
Second Quarter
    CLE-Jurevicius 17-yd. pass from Anderson (Dawson kick)
    CIN-Houshmandzadeh 23-yd. pass from Palmer (Graham kick)
    CLE-Jurevicius 9-yd. pass from Anderson (Dawson kick)
    CIN-C. Johnson 22-yd. pass from Palmer (Graham kick)
    CLE-Winslow 25-yd. pass from Anderson (Dawson kick)
Third Quarter
    CIN-Graham 20-yd. FG
    CLE-Edwards 34-yd. pass from Anderson (Dawson kick)
    CIN-C. Johnson 14-yd. pass from Palmer (Graham kick)

CLE-Lewis 66-yd. run (Dawson kick)
CIN-Houshmandzadeh 5-yd. pass from Palmer (Graham kick)
Fourth Quarter
CLE-Edwards 37-yd. pass from Anderson (Dawson kick)
CLE-Dawson 18-yd. FG
CIN-Holt 7-yd. pass from Palmer (Graham kick)

PASSING
CIN-Palmer 33–50–2–401
CLE-Anderson 20–33–1–328

RUSHING
CIN-R.Johnson 23–118, Palmer 2–10, Perry 1–9
CLE-Lewis 28–215, Cribbs 1–11, Vickers 1–0

RECEIVING
CIN-C. Johnson 11–209, Houshmandzadeh 8–69, Holt 5–52, R. Johnson 4–33,
    Green 1–18, Kelly 1–8, Perry 1–7, Coats 1–4, Watson 1–1
CLE-Edwards 8–146, Winslow 6–100, Jurevicius 4–44, Heiden 1–27, Vickers
    1–1

#39

BROWNS 28, PITTSBURGH STEELERS 23
OCTOBER 24, 1993

Metcalf to the Rescue

By Thursday, it looked like Eric Metcalf wasn't even going to play.

The Browns' versatile running back/kick returner had sprained a knee returning a punt the prior Sunday in Cincinnati and hadn't practiced all week. He finally tested his wobbly knee on Friday but was still questionable for what was being hyped as the biggest Browns-Steelers game in a decade.

Cleveland and Pittsburgh were tied for first in the AFC Central, with the winner of their Week Seven showdown taking sole possession of first place into the second half of the season. Though it would mark the first time in ten years the teams would play with first place on the line, the rivalry itself hadn't cooled. "When I came to Cleveland," third-year coach Bill Belichick said that week, "I heard the Pittsburgh game was a matter of life and death. But, I soon found out it's more than that."

While most expected the Steelers, defending division champs, to once again be in the mix in 1993, the Browns had gotten off to a surprising 4–2 start despite a brewing quarterback controversy. Hometown favorite Bernie Kosar had officially been demoted to backup duties in Week Six, as Belichick gave Vinny Testaverde his first start in a Cleveland uniform. Testaverde was effective in leading the Browns to an eleven-point victory over the Bengals, but many fans were perturbed at Belichick's treatment of Kosar—especially since the decision seemed to be based more on their clashing football philosophies than Kosar's performances. While the 1993 season promised to be interesting, the Kosar-Belichick rift loomed over the Browns' quick start like a rain cloud over a parade. But there were no clouds to speak of when the Browns and Steelers lined up for a late 4 p.m. start at Cleveland Stadium.

Drenched in late October sunlight, the Browns surged to a lead early in the second quarter on a pair of huge plays. First, wideout Michael Jackson turned a simple out-pattern pass into a 62-yard touchdown. Then, after a defensive stop, Metcalf struck. He fielded a Mark Royals punt at the Cleveland nine yard line and bobbed and weaved his way through the Pittsburgh coverage team, not stopping until he reached the end zone after a 91-yard return—the longest in team history. The touchdown put the Browns up 14–0 and sent the sellout Stadium crowd into hysterics.

The Steelers fought back, however, and tied the game at halftime on a pair of Barry Foster touchdown runs. They then took the lead early in the third quarter. The Browns responded with a long drive capped by a short Testaverde scoring pass, but the Steelers came right back with a pair of Gary Anderson field goals, the second putting Pittsburgh ahead 23–21 with 7:51 left in the game.

On the next Cleveland series, Testaverde was blasted by Pittsburgh linebacker Kevin Greene and was forced to the sideline with a separated shoulder. After an exchange of punts, the Browns defense came up with a huge third-down stop, forcing another Royals punt with just over two minutes remaining. The dramatic backdrop was in place. "With Bernie stepping in, everybody knows he runs the two-minute drill with the best of them," Metcalf said later. "That's what I was thinking about—that we were still going to win this game." It would be up to Kosar, the embattled hometown hero, to win the game and salvage his career.

But Metcalf never gave him the chance.

Royals's punt traveled fifty-three yards, sending Metcalf back to his own twenty-five. The elusive scatback from Texas darted through an opening and angled toward the sideline, where he found daylight. He glided smoothly along the Browns bench, where teammates leapt into the air to watch his progress. "I saw it from ten feet in the air," said tight end Brian Kinchen. "I was like a kangaroo." Thanks to two key blocks near midfield, Metcalf weaved into the end zone and up the small grass hill into the waiting embrace of the jubilant Dawg Pound, capping off a 75-yard punt return that gave the Browns a 28–23 lead with 2:05 to play. His teammates piled on top of him in the end zone as the Stadium crowd exploded. For the first time in years, Browns radio announcer Nev Chandler jubilantly labeled Cleveland Stadium "Pandemonium Palace."

It marked the first time in Browns history and only the eighth time any NFL player had ever returned two punts for touchdowns in the same game. "Metcalf was all instinct," *Plain Dealer* columnist Bud Shaw wrote, "instinct topped off at the gas pump with adrenaline." A minute later, Browns safety Stevon Moore forced a fumble at the Pittsburgh forty-nine yard line that Cleveland recovered to clinch the victory. While it was an essential play, Metcalf was the hero in the end, calling it the most emotional game of his career.

The Browns had captured sole possession of first place, and the stage appeared set for a memorable second half of the season, but the win over the Steelers turned out to be the final bright spot of 1993. Two weeks later, Belichick cut Kosar, sending shock waves across Northeast Ohio. The Browns only managed two more wins, finishing 7–9 after two of the most miserable months in Cleveland sports history.

In the shadow of Metcalf's unforgettable October evening, one can only wonder if Kosar could have won the Pittsburgh game with a last-minute drive and if so, would history have unfolded differently?

Perhaps, but certainly not as dazzlingly.

	1	2	3	4	
Steelers	0	14	6	3	=23
Browns	0	14	7	7	=28

Second Quarter
   CLE-Jackson 62-yd. pass from Testaverde (Stover kick)
   CLE-Metcalf 91-yd. punt return (Stover kick)
   PIT-Foster 4-yd. run (Anderson kick)
   PIT-Foster 1-yd. run (Anderson kick)
Third Quarter
   PIT-Anderson 30-yd. FG
   CLE-Wolfley 4-yd. pass from Testaverde (Stover kick)
   PIT-Anderson 46-yd. FG
Fourth Quarter
   PIT-Anderson 30-yd. FG
   CLE-Metcalf 75-yd. punt return (Stover kick)

RUSHING
PIT-Foster 28–87, O'Donnell 1–11, Hoge 2–9, Mills 2–(-7)
CLE-Metcalf 7–53, Vardell 7–19, Baldwin 2–13, Testaverde 1–9, Hoard 1–3,
   Kosar 4–1

PASSING
PIT-O'Donnell 25–39–1–355
CLE-Testaverde 9–14–0–167, Kosar 1–2–0–7

RECEIVING
PIT-Green 6–108, Graham 5–89, Stone 5–54, Hoge 4–43, Foster 3–40, Thigpen 1–13, Mills 1–8
CLE-Jackson 2–106, Hoard 2–20, Metcalf 3–18, Smith 1–17, Wolfley 2–13

#38

The Start of the Whole Thing

The season may have been only seven weeks old, but it had already been a roller-coaster ride. And it was about to take a severe dip.

After dropping three of their first five games, the Browns were about to drop below .500 once again with an unacceptable home loss to the mediocre Green Bay Packers. Unless the Browns could pull off some kind of miracle in the final twenty-five seconds, they would drop to 3–4 and all but eliminate any playoff aspirations they might have brought with them into the 1980 season.

They'd earned the nickname "Kardiac Kids" for their array of fantastic finishes over the previous two seasons—both in victory and defeat—but on this overcast afternoon on the lakefront, they'd essentially handed the game to Green Bay with a pretty little bow wrapped around it. The Browns surged to a 13–0 advantage midway through the third quarter, but the lead would have been more were it not for a handful of mental mistakes that cost the team points. Suddenly, the tide turned. The Packers scored two touchdowns in three minutes to take a lead into the fourth quarter then appeared to put the icing on the cake when quarterback Lynn Dickey hit wide receiver James Lofton for a 26-yard score to make it 21–13 Green Bay with just over seven minutes remaining. "I definitely felt it slipping away a little," Browns quarterback Brian Sipe would say later, "and I won't say I didn't think, 'What if' a few times, because it would have been such a shame to lose."

True to form, the Browns didn't give up, cutting the margin to one two plays later with a scoring pass from Brian Sipe to Ozzie Newsome after veteran running back Calvin Hill turned an innocent screen pass into a 50-yard gain on the previous play. The Browns still had a shot with 6:55 left, but then the Packers began to slide shut the window of opportunity.

On its ensuing possession, Green Bay drove from its sixteen yard line to the Cleveland forty-three, chewing up four minutes. The Pack faced third-and-seven with just over two minutes remaining, and a first down would wrap up victory. It appeared they'd get it when tailback Eddie Lee Ivery took a pitch around right end and crossed the forty yard line, but Browns linebackers Robert L. Jackson and Charlie Hall dragged him down at the thirty-seven, one yard short of the marker. Green Bay punted, and the Browns took over at their own thirteen with 1:53 left.

Sipe, playing with a gimpy knee, battered ribs, and a sore wrist, hit Hill for fifteen yards then scrambled for nine yards. Fullback Mike Pruitt broke free for an 11-yard gain, and then Sipe hit Hill for sixteen more to the Packer thirty-six yard line. The crowd began to titter, sensing the Browns were just one first down away from game-winning field-goal range. However, the red-hot Cleveland offense stalled. Cody Risien was called for holding, pushing the Browns back to the Green Bay forty-six, then Sipe threw two straight incompletions. It set up third-and-twenty with twenty-five seconds left.

As Sipe stepped up to the line of scrimmage, he couldn't believe his eyes. The Packers were preparing to blitz rather than play it safe. And for a veteran quarterback like Sipe—in the middle of the finest season of his career—it was like throwing raw meat to a wild dog. He dropped back and lobbed the football downfield in the direction of wideout Dave Logan, who was single-covered by Packer rookie cornerback Mark Lee. "I just took seven steps backwards, lobbed the ball and let Dave play basketball," Sipe said. Logan—who had been drafted by the NBA's Kansas City Kings coming out of college—leaped over Lee to catch the pass at the nineteen yard line and, as the Stadium crowd of 75,000-plus erupted around him, skipped into the end zone for the game-winning touchdown with sixteen seconds showing on the clock.

Logan's teammates piled on top of him to the point that he almost lost consciousness. Led by a battered Sipe, who had somehow overcome three different injuries to throw for 391 yards, the Browns had turned sure defeat into sudden victory and saved the season in the process. In retrospect, they'd done even more than that.

"That's when we really became the Kardiac Kids," safety Thom Darden said years later. "Everyone thought we were going to lose that game. That started the whole thing."

"That made everyone believe," agreed offensive lineman Joe DeLamielleure. "We knew we had something going here."

And that something turned out to be the most memorable single season in

Browns history. October 19, 1980, was the day the Kardiac Kids became more
than just a nickname.

	1	2	3	4	
Packers	0	0	14	7	=21
Browns	0	10	3	13	=26

Second Quarter
   CLE-Cockroft 40-yd. FG
   CLE-M. Pruitt 1-yd. run (Cockroft kick)
Third Quarter
   CLE-Cockroft 42-yd. FG
   GB-Dickey 7-yd. run (Birney kick)
   GB-Ellis 1-yd. run (Birney kick)
Fourth Quarter
   GB-Lofton 26-yd. pass from Dickey (Birney kick)
   CLE-Newsome 19-yd. pass from Sipe (Cockroft kick)
   CLE-Logan 46-yd. pass from Sipe (kick failed)

RUSHING
GB-Ellis 9–32, Middleton 13–25, Atkins 5–14, Ivery 7–11, Dickey 3–8
CLE-M. Pruitt 16–43, Sipe 2–33, White 7–13, G. Pruitt 1–(-2)

PASSING
GB-Dickey 17–22–3–230
CLE-Sipe 24–39–0–391

RECEIVING
GB-Lofton 8–136, Thompson 1–43, Ellis 2–22, Ivery 1–12, Middleton 4–11,
   Coffman 1–6
CLE-Hill 5–94, Rucker 5–81, M. Pruitt 6–61, Newsome 5–60, Logan 2–52,
   G. Pruitt 1–43

BROWNS 28, HOUSTON OILERS 23
DECEMBER 18, 1988

Strock Around the Clock

The monumental expectations for the 1988 Browns had all but evaporated, and now, the only thing standing between a playoff berth and outright disaster was their fourth-string quarterback.

Thirty-eight-year-old Don Strock was on a Florida golf course, happily enjoying his well-deserved retirement after a fourteen-year career as a backup quarterback when the Browns came calling in mid-September. After losing Bernie Kosar and backup Gary Danielson to injury in the first two games of a season in which the Browns were predicted by many to cruise to the Super Bowl, the Browns desperately needed someone—*anyone*—with NFL experience to back up third-stringer-turned-starter Mike Pagel. And it proved to be a wise decision, since Pagel himself went down with a separated shoulder four weeks later, improbably propelling the ageless Strock into the starting lineup. He led the Browns to a do-or-die win over Philadelphia in Week Seven, which kept their playoff hopes alive until Kosar returned.

But in Week Fifteen, Kosar was injured again in a Monday-night loss in Miami. It would now be up to Strock to propel the 9–6 Browns to victory over the red-hot Houston Oilers in the season finale at frosty Cleveland Stadium. Strock's mission was clear: manage the game, don't make any mistakes, and let the Browns defense and running game lead the way. But by halftime, that plan was in tatters.

The usually dependable Strock played the worst thirty minutes of his career, throwing three interceptions—one of which was returned for a touchdown— and fumbling away another scoring opportunity in the final seconds of the half. The Oilers, led by coach Jerry Glanville (who'd made a handful of colorfully disparaging remarks about Cleveland the week before), built a comfortable

23–7 lead midway through the third quarter and, as snow flurries began to blanket the chewed-up Stadium turf, it appeared the Browns were finished.

But Strock rebounded from his nightmarish first half and caught fire. Using safe, effective passes, he guided the Browns to a pair of touchdowns to close the margin to two points early in the fourth. Then, with the snow accumulating, the Cleveland defense again stymied the Oilers, and Strock and Co. took over at their own eleven and picked up where they left off. After converting on a critical fourth-and-three, they reached the Houston twenty-two yard line, where Strock called for an audible and hit streaking wideout Webster Slaughter over the middle for a touchdown pass that gave the Browns their first lead with 6:23 to play. After another defensive stop, the Browns regained possession, and thanks to a pair of crucial third-down conversions, Strock ran out all but the final twenty seconds to clinch Cleveland's fourth straight playoff berth and complete one of the finest individual comebacks in NFL history.

After almost being run out of town in the first half, Strock rallied to hit on sixteen of twenty-two passes for 212 yards in the second half to become the toast of Cleveland. "This was a great game for the Cleveland Browns, and I'm glad I was a part of it," he said in the jubilant locker room.

In keeping with the city's spirit of ingenuity, a song titled "Strock Around the Clock" (an homage to Bill Haley's 1954 classic "Rock Around the Clock") was quickly written and recorded the following week. It received heavy airplay on Cleveland radio stations as the team prepared for its Wild Card Game rematch with the Oilers six days later.

But Strock didn't get a chance to play the hero the second time around. Appropriately, the star-crossed Browns suffered their fifth quarterback injury of the season when Strock jammed his wrist on the first play of the second quarter and was forced out of the game. He would never again take a snap in the NFL, but his legacy would be preserved with his season-saving performance on a snowy Sunday on the shores of Lake Erie.

	1	2	3	4	
Oilers	10	6	7	0	=23
Browns	0	7	7	14	=28

First Quarter
HOU-Zendejas 39-yd. FG
HOU-Bryant 36-yd. INT return (Zendejas kick)
Second Quarter
CLE-Perry 10-yd. fumble return (Bahr kick)

HOU-Zendejas 42-yd. FG

HOU-Zendejas 35-yd. FG

Third Quarter

HOU-Jeffires 7-yd. pass from Moon (Zendejas kick)

CLE-Byner 2-yd. pass from Strock (Bahr kick)

Fourth Quarter

CLE-Byner 2-yd. run (Bahr kick)

CLE-Slaughter 22-yd. pass from Strock (Bahr kick)

RUSHING

HOU-Rozier 10–17, Highsmith 4–12, Pinkett 6–10, White 1–0, Moon 2–(-2)

CLE-Fontenot 13–42, Byner 19–36, Strock 1–0

PASSING

HOU-Moon 20–35–0–287

CLE-Strock 25–42–3–326

RECEIVING

HOU-Givins 6–119, Hill 5–59, Highsmith 2–44, Jeffires 1–8, Pinkett 3–34, Rozier 3–24

CLE-Slaughter 6–136, Langhorne 6–68, Weathers 3–47, Byner 5–31, Fontenot 3–29, Newsome 1–13, Brennan 1–2

#36

Intrastate Warfare

Though the Cleveland Browns and Cincinnati Bengals had never played an actual game, there already was a rivalry bubbling under the surface just waiting to erupt. On a cool, overcast afternoon at Cleveland Stadium, it finally did.

At the maelstrom of the storm was sixty-two-year-old Paul Brown, who had been a pivotal figure in the foundation of both franchises. Returning to Cleveland for only the second time in the seven years since Art Modell had fired him, the veteran coach tried to downplay the massive hype surrounding the contest. "I've been through so many Sunday afternoons and so many games, it will just be another game," he said that week in a tone that was almost believable. Everyone knew Brown would love nothing more than to march into his old stomping grounds and hand Modell an embarrassing loss.

Even the Cleveland fans, who had been in an uproar when Brown was fired, had now turned against their team's namesake. After the Bengals defeated the Browns in an exhibition game at Riverfront Stadium in late August, Blanton Collier jogged to midfield for the traditional handshake with the opposing coach. But Brown had already left for the locker room, continuing his long-standing custom not to shake hands after a game. Still, the incident took on a life of its own and soon trickled down to the players. "It hurt me when Paul did that to him," Browns defensive end Jack Gregory said. "That's why I'm going to try my damnedest Sunday."

A standing-room-only crowd of 83,520—the fifteenth straight home crowd of better than 80,000 at the Stadium—was wired from the get-go as the teams began what would become a ferocious battle. Ironically, with the Bengals' plain orange helmets and dark jerseys, fans had to continually remind themselves which team was which. "It looked as if it might have been an intra-squad game," Brown said later.

The Browns, favored by ten points, quickly fell behind by ten before clawing back. Defensive end Walter Johnson trapped Bengals quarterback Virgil Carter in the end zone for a safety—one of five Cleveland sacks on the day—then Leroy Kelly broke free on a 55-yard run that set up Cleveland's first touchdown, cutting the margin to one.

The Bengals surged back ahead by two scores when defensive end Royce Berry returned a Bill Nelsen fumble fifty-eight yards for a score, but the Browns responded with a short Nelsen–to–Milt Morin touchdown pass to make it 17–16 at the half. A field goal gave Cincinnati a four-point advantage heading into the fourth quarter before the Browns vaulted ahead on a 1-yard Kelly touchdown run. Cleveland defensive back Erich Barnes then picked off a Carter pass and returned it to the Cincinnati six yard line, setting up another score on a short run by Bo Scott that put the Browns up by ten. Appropriately, the Bengals didn't quit, pulling back within three, but the Browns converted on a pair of critical third downs in the final minutes to melt the clock and preserve victory. The win pushed them into sole possession of first place in the brand-new AFC Central Division and began a new chapter in Browns history.

As Paul Brown left the field (again without shaking Collier's hand), the Stadium crowd booed him mercilessly. Yet he was magnanimous in defeat. "I was proud of the Browns," he said afterward. "They showed tremendous poise out there today. You have to hand it to them."

Despite the off-field graciousness, a new chapter in both teams' histories had begun. The on- and off-field intensity made it clear the Bengals had replaced the New York Giants and the Pittsburgh Steelers as the Browns' archenemy. "Two hundred and forty-four miles separate Cleveland from Cincinnati—fortunately," the *Plain Dealer*'s Edward Whelan wrote. "If the two were any closer, there might be intrastate warfare."

	1	2	3	4	
Bengals	10	7	3	7	=27
Browns	2	14	0	14	=30

First Quarter
   CIN-Muhlmann 50-yd. FG
   CIN-Phillips 2-yd. run (Muhlmann kick)
   CLE-Safety: Johnson tackled Carter in end zone

Second Quarter
   CLE-Kelly 3-yd. pass from Nelsen (Cockroft kick)
   CIN-Berry 58-yd. fumble return (Muhlmann kick)
   CLE-Morin 4-yd. pass from Nelsen (Cockroft kick)
Third Quarter
   CIN-Muhlmann 23-yd. FG
Fourth Quarter
   CLE-Kelly 1-yd. run (Cockroft kick)
   CLE-Scott 1-yd. run (Cockroft kick)
   CIN-Thomas 16-yd. pass from Carter (Muhlmann kick)

RUSHING
CIN-Phillips 13–33, Robinson 6–17, Johnson 1–4
CLE-Kelly 29–84, Scott 10–44, Morin 1–2, Nelsen 1–0

PASSING
CIN-Carter 20–28–1–218
CLE-Nelsen 17–29–1–226

RECEIVING
CIN-Thomas 7–82, Crabtree 3–55, Coslet 3–48, Robinson 3–21, Phillips
   4–12
CLE-Kelly 5–79, Collins 5–65, Morin 4–40, Scott 2–29, Hooker 1–13

#35

BROWNS 19, DALLAS COWBOYS 14
DECEMBER 10, 1994

The One-Inch Upset

Though the Browns were on the brink of clinching their first playoff berth in five years, they weren't getting much respect around the league or even in Cleveland. Most felt their 9–4 record was inflated by a weak schedule, and a lethargic five-turnover, eleven-penalty performance in a home loss to the mediocre New York Giants in Week Fourteen did little to change that thinking. More than knocking the Browns out of first place in the AFC Central, it appeared the Giants loss might prove to be the turning point of the season. A second straight stretch-drive defeat loomed as Cleveland scrambled through a short week of practice before embarking west to take on the Dallas Cowboys, winners of the last two Super Bowls.

The 11–2 Cowboys were obsessed with winning a third straight title and were in a fierce battle with San Francisco to capture home-field advantage through the NFC playoffs. Dallas had become what every NFL team yearned to be. "They have the best offense, the best defense and the best special teams," Browns defensive lineman Michael Dean Perry said. "To tell you the truth, I don't even know why we're going down there," he added jovially, yet there was a layer of truth to the comment. The Browns were ten-point underdogs for their Saturday-afternoon showdown at Texas Stadium, where the Cowboys would play before their sixty-sixth consecutive sellout crowd, either at home or away.

Even before the Browns arrived at the stadium, the day was a nightmare. One of the team buses was involved in a serious collision on the way to Texas Stadium, and several players and coaches were notably rattled. Yet the offense looked focused on its first possession, driving to the Dallas ten yard line, where Vinny Testaverde hit running back Leroy Hoard on a screen pass for what appeared would be a sure touchdown. But Hoard was hit by defensive end

Charles Haley at the one and fumbled into the end zone, where the Cowboys recovered. Thirteen plays later, Dallas went up 7–0, and this spirit-crushing turn of events seemed certain to bury the Browns.

Instead, they came right back to tie the contest on a Testaverde touchdown pass to Michael Jackson on the final play of the first quarter. The defense then recovered a Dallas fumble at midfield. Texas native Matt Stover—who had competed in the Pass, Punt & Kick regional finals at Texas Stadium as a child— kicked the first of what would be four clutch field goals to put the Browns ahead 10–7. There the score remained until early in the fourth quarter when Stover added two more field goals in a three-minute stretch—after Browns corner- back Don Griffin intercepted Dallas quarterback Troy Aikman—to push the Browns' lead to nine. But the Cowboys came right back with a 78-yard drive capped by an Emmitt Smith touchdown run with 6:21 remaining. The stage was set for the unbelievable finish. "It was like a heavyweight fight between two great punchers," Bill Belichick would say later.

After Browns punter Tom Tupa pinned Dallas inside its own ten yard line, the Cleveland defense had its finest moment. It stuffed Smith for a yard gain on third-and-three, and the swaggering Cowboys opted to go for it on fourth-and- two at their own fifteen. Aikman fumbled, and Browns lineman Bill Johnson recovered, setting up Stover's fourth field goal with 1:32 left to make it 19–14. It would once again be up to the Cleveland defense, and once again, it would respond. After Kevin Williams returned the ensuing kickoff to the Cowboy forty-eight yard line, Aikman caught fire, directing Dallas to the Cleveland six with ten seconds left. The Browns' backs were to the wall, and a second straight last-minute loss hovered before them like a specter.

Out of time-outs, Aikman dropped back and slung a pass for tight end Jay Novacek over the middle. Novacek—wide open after Browns linebacker Mike Caldwell blew his coverage on the play—caught the ball at the two yard line and began to turn toward the goal line. But as he did, his feet slipped on the slick Texas Stadium Astroturf, which had sat uncovered during a heavy downpour the night before, and as he lost his footing, Browns safety Eric Turner—playing with his left arm dangling limply from an earlier shoulder injury—slammed into him at the one. When Novacek landed, his shoulders were at the goal line, and his helmet was actually across it. Yet the football remained just shy of it. "When his head hit the ground, it was an inch away from the goal line," Cleveland linebacker Pepper Johnson said. "I've been in games where the ref would call that a touchdown."

The world seemed to stop. The Browns turned to the scoreboard and watched the clock slowly tick down to zero. When it finally did, the Cleveland bench flooded onto the field. "It felt like we won the Super Bowl," cornerback Antonio Langham declared. "We were the giant killers," Pepper Johnson added. "It was like Ali beating up Sonny Liston and shaking up the world." As word of the upset spread across the nation that Saturday night, the Browns were no longer overrated. "I don't think we need to ask for respect anymore," Turner said. "I believe we have it."

	1	2	3	4	
Browns	7	3	0	9	=19
Cowboys	7	0	0	7	=14

First Quarter
   DAL-Smith 7-yd. pass from Aikman (Boniol kick)
   CLE-Jackson 2-yd. pass from Testaverde (Stover kick)
Second Quarter
   CLE-Stover 34-yd. FG
Fourth Quarter
   CLE-Stover 32-yd. FG
   CLE-Stover 43-yd. FG
   DAL-Smith 4-yd. run (Boniol kick)
   CLE-Stover 32-yd. FG

RUSHING
CLE-Hoard 25–99, Metcalf 3–19, Byner 4–8, Baldwin 4–6, Testaverde 2–2
DAL-Smith 26–112, Aikman 1–0

PASSING
CLE-Testaverde 15–25–1–118
DAL-Aikman 21–36–2–188

RECEIVING
CLE-Jackson 6–74, Kinchen 3–13, Metcalf 3–13, Hoard 1–9, Carrier 1–7, Baldwin 1–2
DAL-Irvin 7–88, Harper 2–27, Williams 2–26, Smith 5–22, Johnston 3–15, Novacek 2–10

#34

Changing Their Stripes

In the three decades of their existence, things had never been worse for the Cleveland Browns.

The previous season, 1974, had been the most miserable in their history. Their 4–10 record marked just the second time in twenty-nine years the Browns had suffered through a losing campaign. A new era began the following January when offensive-line coach Forrest Gregg was promoted to replace retiring head coach Nick Skorich, but things got off to a cataclysmic start. The 1975 Browns lost their first nine games, six by fourteen points or more, extending their team-record losing streak to a whopping twelve.

Fans had lost their patience with quarterback Mike Phipps, who had yet to throw a touchdown pass in 1975 and had been booed mercilessly. He was benched in the third quarter of a thirty-point loss to Houston in Week Four in favor of inexperienced backup Brian Sipe and wouldn't start again for a month. "It's time for the fans to forget about the Paul Warfield trade and quit living in the past," Gregg snarled the day after loss number nine. "It's time for them to look toward the future. There really is a light at the end of the tunnel."

But a tenth loss seemed a certainty on a sunshiny November Sunday as the red-hot Cincinnati Bengals rolled into Cleveland Stadium. It was the best Bengal team in the eight-year history of the franchise, and many thought coach Paul Brown might pick up one last championship in his final year on the sideline. At 8–1, Cincinnati was tied with Pittsburgh for first place in the AFC Central and needed a victory to keep pace with the defending Super Bowl champs.

The Bengals were coming off a wild Monday-night victory over Buffalo in which Cincinnati quarterback Ken Anderson had put together the finest game of his career, tossing for 447 yards. "The Browns this week should know how the folks down on the coasts of Florida and Louisiana feel when a hurricane is coming their way," wrote Chuck Heaton. "They know it's coming, but there really isn't much that can be done about it but a few prayers or finding a safer spot."

They were two teams headed in dramatically opposite directions. A blowout seemed imminent. But the opening kickoff forecasted an unusual day. Browns wide receiver Billy Lefear sprinted ninety-two yards down the sideline before getting tripped up at the Bengal two yard line. Perhaps appropriately for the '75 Browns, Lefear broke his right leg on the tackle and would never play another down in the NFL. On the next play, running back Greg Pruitt covered the last two yards—the first of what would be a combined 304 for Pruitt on the day—to give the Browns a 6–0 advantage.

The Bengals roared back and surged to a 20–9 lead on a pair of long Anderson scoring passes. After a Don Cockroft field goal on the final play of the first half brought the Browns to within eight, Cincinnati pushed the lead back to eleven with a long scoring march on the first series of the third quarter. The drive was a costly one, however, as Anderson was drilled by Browns defensive end Jerry Sherk and was forced to the sideline with a bruised chest.

With Anderson out, the momentum began to shift. Another Cockroft field goal made it 23–15. Then, early in the fourth period, the Browns faced third-and-three at the Bengal five. Phipps fired a lofty pass into the end zone, and tight end Oscar Roan leapt up seemingly above the crossbar and snagged the football with one hand for a spectacular touchdown catch that pulled the Browns within one. "There was no way I thought I could reach it," Roan would say later. "I just jumped for it, and something helped me up."

After the Cleveland defense forced a three-and-out, the Browns took the lead on a 13-yard Phipps touchdown pass to Pruitt, who darted through Bengal defenders like a pinball on his way to the end zone. But the game was still in doubt until the final moments, when Browns defensive back Jim Hill intercepted a John Reaves pass at the Cleveland forty-four yard line and returned it fifty-six yards for the clinching touchdown. The Browns had rallied to score twenty-three unanswered points and sabotage the Bengals' hopes for a division title.

As the final gun sounded, the Stadium crowd poured onto the field. Many fans mobbed Phipps, who had played the finest game of his embattled career. Hobbling on a sore foot, he'd completed twenty-three of thirty-six passes for 298 yards.

After picking up his first victory as head coach, Gregg was presented the game ball by his players. The longest losing streak in team history had evaporated into the crisp autumn air with one of the franchise's most surprising and satisfying victories. Suddenly, as Heaton wrote, "now the town is smiling again, and the football season doesn't seem long enough."

	1	2	3	4	
Bengals	13	7	3	0	=23
Browns	9	3	3	20	=35

First Quarter
CLE-Pruitt 2-yd. run (kick failed)
CLE-Cockroft 27-yd. FG
CIN-Trumpy 35-yd. pass from Anderson (Green kick)
CIN-Fritts 4-yd. run (kick blocked)
Second Quarter
CIN-Curtis 30-yd. pass from Anderson (Green kick)
CLE-Cockroft 32-yd. FG
Third Quarter
CIN-Green 21-yd. FG
CLE-Cockroft 43-yd. FG
Fourth Quarter
CLE-Roan 5-yd. pass from Phipps (Cockroft kick)
CLE-Pruitt 13-yd. pass from Phipps (kick failed)
CLE-Hill 56-yd. INT return (Cockroft kick)

RUSHING
CIN-Elliott 13–35, Williams 4–18, Clark 6–15, Fritts 3–4, Anderson 1–1, Reaves 1–1
CLE-Pruitt 17–121, Pritchett 13–40, Phipps 2–7, Miller 1–(-2)

PASSING
CIN-Anderson 13–20–0–292, Reaves 4–11–1–68
CLE-Phipps 23–36–0–298

RECEIVING
CIN-Joiner 7–200, Curtis 2–77, Trumpy 2–44, Elliott 3–21, Williams 1–19, Clark 1–7, Coslet 1–2
CLE-Pruitt 7–106, Holden 5–93, Rucker 6–64, Roan 3–25, Pritchett 2–10

BROWNS 24, BALTIMORE RAVENS 14
OCTOBER 21, 2001

A Game That Soothed the Soul

While Browns fans rejoiced at the triumphant return of their team in 1999, beneath the surface was a potent coating of bitterness and anger which only got stronger and more consuming as the expansion Browns suffered through back-to-back hellish seasons. They lost twenty-seven of their first thirty-two games, many in miserable and unspeakable fashion.

But Clevelanders' frustration peaked at a white-hot level of intensity in January 2001 when Art Modell hoisted the Vince Lombardi Trophy after his Baltimore Ravens had cruised to a victory over the New York Giants in Super Bowl XXXV. After decades of watching Modell tinker and toy with their beloved team, *his* ultimate dream had come true just over five years after betraying the Cleveland fans that had tolerated him for so long. Making matters worse, that Baltimore team had been put together by former Browns Hall of Fame tight end Ozzie Newsome, now Baltimore's general manager, and coached by yet another specter of the Browns' past.

Brian Billick had been offered the Cleveland head-coaching position early in 1999 but decided to hear other options first and took the Ravens job later that week—infuriating the Browns' fledgling front office and further crippling Cleveland's first season back. Billick would then go on to turn around the mediocre Ravens in two short seasons, easily beating the Browns four times along the way by a combined score of 114–26.

As the loudmouth Ravens began 2001 talking about a dynasty, the Browns started the campaign with newfound energy under first-year coach Butch Davis. Cleveland won three of its first four and stood at 3–2 going into a Week Six showdown with the Ravens at Cleveland Browns Stadium. Though visiting Baltimore held the same record, the Ravens were seven-and-a-half-point favorites, mostly on the reputation of their dominating defense, which was ranked second in the NFL and tops against the run. The Browns, meanwhile, had managed just thirty-four yards on the ground the previous week in a loss in Cincinnati, and had yet to find a bona-fide number one running back in the three years since their return.

Rather than being intimidated by the defending world champions in the early going, the Browns took it right to them. Eccentric running back Ben Gay returned the opening kickoff forty-two yards, setting the tone for a surprising opening drive that ended three plays later when tailback James Jackson took a handoff and sprinted through a gaping hole in the impenetrable Baltimore front for an 11-yard touchdown run. The Browns defense kept Baltimore in check through the remainder of the half, and Cleveland carried a 10–6 margin into the third quarter. That's when the game turned upside down.

Midway through the period, Browns quarterback Tim Couch capped an 80-yard drive with a 28-yard touchdown pass to wideout Kevin Johnson that made it 17–6. Baltimore quarterback Elvis Grbac, a Cleveland native, fumbled moments later, and the Browns recovered. On the next snap, Couch went for the throat, hitting rookie wide receiver Quincy Morgan with a perfect strike for a 36-yard score that put the game away at 24–6. After Morgan's only catch of the day, he leapt over the wall separating the field from the stands and was absorbed by the long-suffering denizens of the Dawg Pound.

As heavy rain swept through downtown Cleveland in the fourth quarter, the Browns hung on for a 24–14 triumph over the defending Super Bowl champions. Though many fans had scampered for cover when the rain started, *Plain Dealer* columnist Bill Livingston noted, "the roar from those who were left was still big enough to swallow up years of anger, hurt and disappointment."

It was the Browns' first-ever victory over the Baltimore Ravens, bringing closure to a six-year horror story. It was a game, as Livingston wrote, that soothed the soul.

But, broadcaster Doug Dieken put it best: "Cleveland—this win's for you."

	1	2	3	4	
Ravens	0	6	0	8	=14
Browns	7	3	14	0	=24

First Quarter
CLE-Jackson 11-yd. run (Dawson kick)
Second Quarter
BAL-Stover 21-yd. FG

CLE-Dawson 33-yd. FG

BAL-Stover 38-yd. FG

Third Quarter

CLE-Johnson 28-yd. pass from Couch (Dawson kick)

CLE-Morgan 36-yd. pass from Couch (Dawson kick)

Fourth Quarter

BAL-Ismail 22-yd. pass from Cunningham (Ismail pass from Cunningham)

RUSHING

BAL-Ayanbadejo 9–48, Brookins 13–46, Allen 3–12, Cunningham 1–5, Williams 1–2

CLE-Jackson 24–77, Couch 4–10, White 1–1

PASSING

BAL-Grbac 16–20–2–142, Cunningham 11–25–0–120

CLE-Couch 11–18–0–149

RECEIVING

BAL-Ismail 7–85, Stokely 5–68, Sharpe 6–61, Brookins 3–24, Ayanbadejo 5–20, Gash 1–4

CLE-Johnson 3–47, Morgan 1–36, Santiago 1–27, Jackson 2–13, Sellers 1–12, Northcutt 1–11, Shea 1–2, White 1–1

#32

BROWNS 30, BALTIMORE COLTS 20
OCTOBER 20, 1968

Regaining Their Pride

By the third week of October 1968, it appeared as if the Browns—once the mightiest team in football—had lost their identity.

It had been nearly six years since Art Modell had dismissed Paul Brown as head coach, almost three since future Hall of Fame running back Jim Brown decided to give up football at the peak of his gridiron career. Instead of enjoying him bowl over tacklers on the football field, if Cleveland fans wanted to see Brown now, they'd have to head to a local movie theater to watch him star with Diahann Carroll in *The Split,* which opened that Friday. And by then, it looked like any hopes the Browns might have of once again becoming a championship-caliber team seemed just as realistic as the plot from one of Jim Brown's movies.

After winning an NFL title under new coach Blanton Collier in 1964 then reaching the title game again in Jim Brown's final year of 1965, the next two seasons were far from memorable. Cleveland posted back-to-back 9–5 records—relatively disappointing considering the rich history of the franchise. They finished second to Dallas in the Eastern Conference in '66 then won the mediocre new Century Division in '67 but were then blasted by the Cowboys in the conference championship.

A month into the 1968 season, it appeared the Browns were on course for a third straight ho-hum campaign. They'd dropped three of their first five games, including lopsided losses to playoff perennials Dallas and Los Angeles and a disheartening home loss to division rival St. Louis in Week Five. A fourth loss appeared a sure thing with a trip to Baltimore looming. The 5–0 Colts had become the finest team in football, allowing just fifty-eight points all season under a defensive coaching staff that included Chuck Noll—less than a year away from taking the head job in Pittsburgh. Baltimore head coach Don Shula, just about to enter the prime of a legendary career, had the best record of any NFL coach since taking over the Colts in 1963, losing just seventeen games in six years. Aging but still potent quarterback Earl Morrall—who joined the team midway through the preseason—led the league in passing, with future Hall of Famer Johnny Unitas backing him up.

Accordingly, the Browns were whopping seventeen-point underdogs going into a game that seemed to mark the crossroads not only for the 1968 season but for the franchise as a whole. "That's more than just another football game coming up for the Browns on Sunday in Baltimore," Chuck Heaton wrote. "It's an opportunity—perhaps the last one this season—to regain some of the stature Cleveland pro football teams of the past enjoyed."

"If the Browns can upset Baltimore," Heaton continued, "they once again will enjoy some of the prestige of other campaigns. A victory, or even a close contest, and the fans will resume their love affair with the guys in shoulder pads.

"Another real thomping . . . will be convincing evidence that this is a second-rate team. Even a repeat as Century Division champions would do little to erase the image."

The Browns came out strong on a sunny autumn afternoon at Memorial Stadium, driving into Baltimore territory on their first possession. Though rookie kicker Don Cockroft was short on a 47-yard field-goal attempt, it was clear these were not the same Browns who had looked so lethargic over the previous five weeks. A key factor was the return of running back Ernie Green, who had rushed for better than 700 yards in each of the previous two seasons. Green, who had yet to play in '68 because of a preseason injury, would only pick up twelve yards on five carries on the day, but he proved to be the spark the Browns offense desperately needed.

Minutes later, defensive tackle Jim Kanicki forced a Morrall fumble, and end Jim Houston recovered at the Colts thirty-seven yard line, setting up a short Bill Nelsen–to–Leroy Kelly touchdown pass. Cleveland native Tom Matte equalized matters with a 23-yard scoring run in the second quarter, but the Browns took back the lead on a six-yard touchdown pass from Nelsen to wideout Paul Warfield, capping an 81-yard drive.

Though the Colts trailed by just seven, Shula decided to replace Morrall with Unitas to start the second half. Johnny U's first toss was picked off by defensive back Mike Howell, which led to a third Nelsen touchdown pass, this one to wide receiver Eppie Barney on a gutsy fourth-down call to make it 21–7. Baltimore stayed within reach with a pair of third-quarter field goals, but the Browns pulled away in the final quarter. A four-yard touchdown run by Kelly, who rushed for 130 yards on the day, and a short Cockroft field goal put the contest out of reach. The final was 30–20, Browns—the biggest upset of the NFL season. As it turned out, it would be the Colts' only loss of 1968.

"It was just like glorious old times for the Browns yesterday," Heaton wrote under the front-page headline, "BROWNS REGAIN THEIR PRIDE."

It was the beginning of an eight-game winning streak that would carry Cleveland to not only another division title and a second straight playoff berth but also back-to-back NFL Championship Game appearances—all begun on a crisp October afternoon in Baltimore.

"It was a do-or-die game for them," Matte said. "They did the job."

	1	2	3	4	
Browns	7	7	7	9	=30
Colts	0	7	6	7	=20

First Quarter
CLE-Kelly 2-yd. pass from Nelsen (Cockroft kick)
Second Quarter
BAL-Matte 23-yd. run (Michaels kick)
CLE-Warfield 6-yd. pass from Nelsen (Cockroft kick)
Third Quarter
CLE-Barney 2-yd. pass from Nelsen (Cockroft kick)
BAL-Michaels 17-yd. FG
BAL-Michaels 32-yd. FG
Fourth Quarter
CLE-Kelly 4-yd. run (kick blocked)
CLE-Cockroft 11-yd. FG
BAL-Richardson 8-yd. pass from Morrall (Michaels kick)

RUSHING
CLE-Kelly 30–130, Nelsen 4–32, Green 5–12, Leigh 4–5
BAL-Matte 13–64, Hill 9–23, Morrall 1–0, Unitas 1–(-6)

PASSING
CLE-Nelsen 15–23–0–137
BAL-Morrall 10–18–1–130, Unitas 1–11–3–12

RECEIVING

CLE-Warfield 5–46, Morin 3–41, Kelly 2–18, Barney 2–17, Green 2–11, Leigh 1–4

BAL-Mackey 3–41, Orr 3–38, Matte 2–37, Hill 2–18, Richardson 1–8

#31

BROWNS 27, PITTSBURGH STEELERS 26
OCTOBER 26, 1980

Pulling Back the Steel Curtain

Sam Rutigliano joked that prior to the 1980 season, he'd put in a request to NFL Commissioner Pete Rozelle that the Browns be permitted to transfer from the AFC Central Division to the Ivy League.

Over the previous two years, the AFC Central had developed into the toughest division in football. Not only had the Browns grown into a playoff contender, but many felt the Houston Oilers had become the league's second-best team. There was no doubt as to which team was at the top of that list—and it also resided in the AFC Central.

Going into the 1980 season, the Pittsburgh Steelers had already assured themselves dynasty status, winning four of the previous six Super Bowls, including the last two. And essentially the same cast of characters had returned, gunning for a fifth ring to start a new decade. The Oilers and Browns, most assumed, would undergo a pitched battle for second place. But by late October, things had changed.

The Steelers, after losing just six games over the previous two years, had looked decidedly human over the first half of the season. Injuries had been a factor, but it appeared the intensity and hunger that had been so prevalent during the Steelers' championship runs had softened. Still, Pittsburgh managed to win four of its first six and was right in the mix for its eighth division crown in nine years.

Meanwhile, the Browns dug an early hole, dropping their first two games and three of their first five before bouncing back to take a 4–3 record into the game of the year. They would host archrival Pittsburgh, looking to snap a seven-game losing streak to the Steelers with first place on the line. A capacity crowd packed into Cleveland Stadium on a dark, unusually cold October

Sunday to see if the Browns would finally stand up to the divisional bully. "If we don't beat the damned Steelers this time," Cleveland general manager Peter Hadhazy said that week, "we might never beat them."

Though the Steelers were handicapped by injury—quarterback Terry Bradshaw, wide receivers Lynn Swann and John Stallworth, running back Franco Harris, and linebacker Jack Lambert wouldn't play—the offense didn't miss a beat. Backup quarterback Cliff Stoudt directed the Steelers to three touchdowns, while the heralded Browns aerial attack sputtered. The Steelers led 20–7 midway through the third quarter when the Browns blew a golden scoring opportunity when they were stuffed shy on fourth-and-three at the Pittsburgh eight yard line. Cleveland showed signs of life when Brian Sipe connected with Greg Pruitt on a short scoring pass to cut the lead to six. But Pittsburgh responded with a lightning-like 71-yard pass from Stoudt to running back Theo Bell to set up another touchdown, making it 26–14 with just over two minutes left in the third quarter. The Browns quickly drove to the Pittsburgh seven, but when Sipe was forced to the sideline with a shoulder stinger, backup Paul McDonald fumbled the next snap, and the Steelers recovered. For all the hype and anticipation, it appeared this wasn't to be Cleveland's day—or season, for that matter.

But, as so often occurred with the Kardiac Kids, the complexion of the game changed rapidly in the fourth quarter. Brian Sipe led the Browns on a 73-yard drive, and they pulled back to within six on a fourth-down scoring pass to Greg Pruitt with 9:21 left. Then, with first place hanging in the balance, the Cleveland defense came up with a huge stop and gave the ball back to the offense. Sipe, enjoying one of the finest games of his career, drove the Browns to the Pittsburgh eighteen yard line, where he crossed up the Steel Curtain defense with a makeshift audible. On third-and-seven, he lofted a pass into the end zone, where streaking Ozzie Newsome caught it right in front of a pack of rabid fans in the bleachers. With Cleveland Stadium literally shaking, the Browns had taken their first lead at 27–26 with 5:38 remaining on Sipe's fourth touchdown pass of the day. Yet, as always with the Kardiac Kids, the game remained in doubt until the final minute.

After a crucial interception in Cleveland territory at the two-minute warning by Ron Bolton and a huge third-down, clock-killing reception by sparingly used wideout Willis Adams, the Browns had secured one of the most thrilling victories in their history. "Cleveland fans have been taking it [from Pittsburgh fans] for years," Browns center Tom DeLeone said afterward. "Now they can start giving it back."

Not only had they picked up their first victory over Pittsburgh in four years, they vaulted into first place and proved that they were finally ready to compete in football's toughest division.

	1	2	3	4	
Steelers	10	3	13	0	=26
Browns	0	7	7	13	=27

First Quarter
PIT-Hawthorne 1-yd. run (Bahr kick)
PIT-Bahr 27-yd. FG
Second Quarter
CLE-Hill 5-yd. pass from Sipe (Cockroft kick)
PIT-Bahr 22-yd. FG
Third Quarter
PIT-Hawthorne 2-yd. run (Bahr kick)
CLE-G. Pruitt 6-yd. pass from Sipe (Cockroft kick)
PIT-Thornton 2-yd. run (kick failed)
Fourth Quarter
CLE-G. Pruitt 7-yd. pass from Sipe (kick failed)
CLE-Newsome 18-yd. pass from Sipe (Cockroft kick)

RUSHING
PIT-Stoudt 4–21, Davis 9–20, Bleier 5–19, Hawthorne 9–16, Thornton 7–11
CLE-M. Pruitt 17–82, G. Pruitt 5–8, White 1–1, Evans 1–0, McDonald 1–0

PASSING
PIT-Stoudt 18–37–1–310
CLE-Sipe 28–46–1–349

RECEIVING
PIT-Bell 4–125, Smith 4–75, Sweeney 2–49, Bleier 4–33, Grossman 1–13, Hawthorne 2–11, Cunningham 1–4
CLE-Logan 8–131, G. Pruitt 8–71, Newsome 4–55, Rucker 3–47, Hill 2–20, Adams 1–10, White 1–10, M. Pruitt 1–5

Above: Cleveland's Dub Jones stretches for extra yardage during a classic Browns-Giants matchup in October 1951. The New York defender in the center is Tom Landry, who would go on to become a Hall of Fame coach with the Dallas Cowboys. Cleveland State University Library's *Cleveland Press* Collection.

Left: Less than two months after being cut by San Francisco, new Cleveland kicker Matt Bahr (center) booted a game-winning field goal to hand the eventual Super Bowl–champ 49ers their only home loss of the 1981 season. Cleveland State University Library's *Cleveland Press* Collection.

The intensity on the face of Cleveland tight end Milt Morin reflects the fierce rivalry born between the Browns and Cincinnati Bengals upon their first meeting in 1970. Cleveland Public Library.

Above: A last-minute field goal in the snow by Giants kicker Pat Summerall at Yankee Stadium on December 14, 1958, stunned the Browns and forced a playoff for the Eastern Division crown. Cleveland State University Library's *Cleveland Press* Collection.

Left: Jim Hill of the Browns intercepts a pass to clinch an incredible upset by the 0–9 Browns over the 8–1 Cincinnati Bengals on November 23, 1975. Cleveland State University Library's *Cleveland Press* Collection.

Browns linebacker Wayne Meylan drags Cowboys running back Calvin Hill into the
Cotton Bowl mud during a Cleveland playoff rout of Dallas on December 28, 1969.
Cleveland State University Library's *Cleveland Press* Collection.

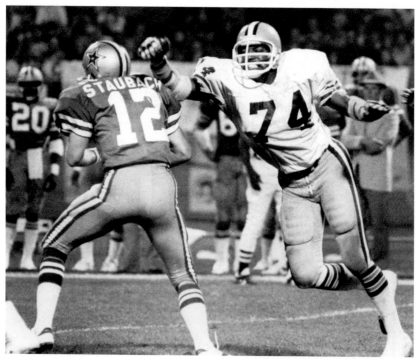

Cleveland lineman Mike St. Clair pursues legendary Dallas quarterback Roger Staubach
during the Browns' dynamic Monday-night victory over the iconic Cowboys on September 24, 1979. Cleveland State University Library's *Cleveland Press* Collection.

Left: Mike Phipps (left) raises his arms in triumph while kicker Don Cockroft bows in disbelief after Cockroft booted a field goal to defeat archrival Pittsburgh on November 19, 1972. Cleveland State University Library's *Cleveland Press* Collection.

Below: Over the outstretched fingers of Cleveland defenders, Doak Walker's extra-point attempt spins into the history books, providing the Detroit Lions with the winning point in their second straight NFL title-game victory—a 17–16 nail-biter over the Browns on December 27, 1953. Cleveland State University Library's *Cleveland Press* Collection.

Teammates mob Browns linebacker Dale Lindsey (second from right) after he returned an interception for a touchdown in Cleveland's rousing playoff victory over Dallas on December 21, 1968. Cleveland State University Library's *Cleveland Press* Collection.

Fred Morrison topples into the end zone for the seventh of eight Cleveland touchdowns on December 26, 1954, when the Browns avenged back-to-back title-game losses to Detroit with a 56–10 thrashing of the Lions. Cleveland State University Library's *Cleveland Press* Collection.

In the defining moment of his career, Cleveland receiver Gary Collins fights through Baltimore's Bobby Boyd to catch his third touchdown pass in the Browns' stunning 27–0 upset of the Colts in the 1964 NFL Championship. Cleveland State University Library's *Cleveland Press* Collection.

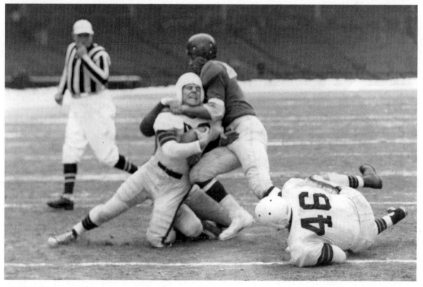

The birth of a rivalry: Rex Bumgardner of the Browns is clotheslined to the ground by Emlen Tunnell of the New York Giants during the historic 1950 American Conference playoff, won by the Browns, 8–3. Cleveland State University Library's *Cleveland Press* Collection.

The greatest moment in Cleveland Browns history—all eyes are on the football as it sails from Lou Groza's foot through the uprights to win an epic NFL Championship over the Los Angeles Rams on Christmas Eve, 1950. Cleveland State University Library's *Cleveland Press* Collection.

#30

Revenge, Batteries, and Two Coats of Paint

It was like a mafia chieftain being extradited to the scene of his most notorious crime.

Though it had been nearly three years since the Denver Broncos had played in Cleveland, no one had forgotten what had happened. The Browns had been on the brink of their first Super Bowl appearance when Denver quarterback John Elway led his team on a 98-yard drive to send the 1986 AFC Championship to overtime, where the Broncos prevailed. Then, the following year in Denver, the Browns again appeared Super Bowl–bound before Earnest Byner's heartbreaking fumble once again punched Denver's ticket to the title game. A Monday-night clash in Cleveland between the teams was wiped out by the players' strike in 1987, so the Browns faithful had to wait thirty-three long months to direct their anger at Elway's Broncos.

But even before Elway arrived in Denver, the Broncos had Cleveland's number. As their 1989 rematch approached, the Browns hadn't beaten Denver in fifteen years, dropping ten straight decisions despite never being completely outmatched. As Ozzie Newsome put it that week, "Weird things happen when we play them." The trend would continue that Sunday.

After having lost all five previous meetings with the athletic and elusive Elway, the Browns defense pinned back their ears and, for the first time, truly targeted Denver's Golden Boy. First-year coach Bud Carson's attack defense had never looked better, sacking Elway four times and allowing just six completions in what would be the worst game of his career. A fumble on a Michael Dean Perry sack led to the game's first score: a picture-perfect touchdown pass from Bernie Kosar to Webster Slaughter that gave the Browns a 7–0 lead. The rout, it appeared, was on. Cleveland dominated play through the first three quarters and clawed to a 13–3 lead. But Elway's talent shone through for one key play—a 68-yard pass to Vance Johnson that set up a field goal and swung the momentum to the Broncos. That's when a handful of double-A batteries altered the course of Browns history.

Backed up at their own four yard line early in the fourth period, the Broncos were huddled in the end zone right in front of the Dog Pound—almost the exact spot where Elway had hit Mark Jackson for the back-breaking touchdown in '86. The bleacherites had been pelting the Broncos with Milk-Bones all day, but this time, the Broncos started getting hit first with raw eggs, then by a rock. When a double-A battery flew into the huddle, referee Tom Dooley decided enough was enough. For just the second time in NFL history, the teams were ordered to switch direction for the remainder of the game. Interestingly, after Denver punted, Broncos coach Dan Reeves lobbied the officials to allow them to switch back since they would now have to go against a steady wind off the lake. The officials denied the request, but in the next few minutes, the Broncos benefited from the switch, as the wind began to change direction, altering the course of a missed 42-yard Matt Bahr field goal that would have given the Browns a comfortable ten-point lead midway through the period.

As was his habit against the Browns, Elway rose to the occasion, hitting running back Steve Sewell for a 53-yard gain to the Cleveland six yard line, then connecting with Johnson for the game-tying touchdown three plays later with less than four minutes remaining. On the next play from scrimmage, the Browns appeared to etch a new chapter in their agonizing rivalry with the Broncos when Kosar was picked off at his own forty-three. Denver marched to the Cleveland eight with 1:49 left, and the sellout crowd was subdued, just waiting for the painful conclusion.

But this time, fate smiled on the previously luckless Browns. On a pitchout designed to simply melt time off the clock and position the Broncos for the game-winning field goal, tailback Sammy Winder was stripped of the football by Browns linebacker Mike Johnson, and cornerback Frank Minnifield recovered at the sixteen yard line. The Browns had received a stay of execution. Yet, rather than play it safe and try to win the game in overtime, they went for the throat. Kosar connected on five clutch passes—the last of which was a makeshift sideline pattern to Slaughter good for a nine-yard gain to the Denver thirty with five seconds left and the Browns out of time-outs. It was close enough to send out Bahr for a 48-yard field-goal attempt on the last play of the game.

Bahr could tell from the moment of contact that the kick had perfect aim. The only question was whether or not it would have enough gas. With the frenzied fans on their feet and holding their collective breath, they watched the kick loft through the air as if in slow motion. It finally reached the goalposts and barely skimmed over the crossbar—clearing it, Bahr said later, by "two coats of paint." Ironically, as the fourth quarter wore on, the wind direction had shifted once again and had made the difference on the game-winning kick.

The "battery incident," as it would come to be known, had inadvertently delivered a "Hitchcock conclusion loaded with irony," as Tony Grossi described it in the *Plain Dealer*. More importantly, it provided a victory Browns fans had been waiting fifteen years for.

"We had to live with 'The Drive' and 'The Fumble,' and I guess it was nice we could get 'The Drive' *and* 'The Fumble' in one game," Bahr said. "I guess you could say we purged the ghost."

	1	2	3	4	
Broncos	0	3	3	7	=13
Browns	7	3	3	3	=16

First Quarter
   CLE-Slaughter 9-yd. pass from Kosar (Bahr kick)
Second Quarter
   DEN-Treadwell 21-yd. FG
   CLE-Bahr 36-yd. FG
Third Quarter
   CLE-Bahr 48-yd. FG
   DEN-Treadwell 26-yd. FG
Fourth Quarter
   DEN-Johnson 7-yd. pass from Elway (Treadwell kick)
   CLE-Bahr 48-yd. FG

RUSHING
DEN-Humphrey 10–44, Alexander 5–17, Winder 8–16
CLE-Kosar 4–33, Metcalf 9–26, Jones 7–21, Manoa 4–21, Redden 1–4, Langhorne 1–(-10)

PASSING
DEN-Elway 6–19–1–198
CLE-Kosar 25–38–1–216

RECEIVING
DEN-Johnson 5–145, Sewell 1–53
CLE-Langhorne 7–67, Slaughter 5–67, Metcalf 5–24, Newsome 3–21, Brennan 2–20, Manoa 1–7, Tillman 1–5, Jones 1–5

BROWNS 18, PITTSBURGH STEELERS 16
OCTOBER 10, 1976

Head Over Heels

Through the entire off-season following the dismal 1975 campaign, the Browns dreamed of finding themselves tied with the two-time defending world-champion Pittsburgh Steelers in mid-October. But when that scenario came to fruition, the Browns were anything but excited.

Cleveland had lost three of its first four games in 1976, not at all surprising after suffering through a 3–11 season the year before. But somehow, Pittsburgh was also 1–3 heading into Week Five after posting a league-best 12–2 mark en route to a Super Bowl X title a year earlier. The Browns and Steelers were tied for last in the AFC Central, two games behind Cincinnati and Houston, and both teams entered their October 10 showdown at Cleveland Stadium feeling a loss would essentially destroy the remainder of the season.

But a doomed season would be nothing new for the Browns, who had dropped sixteen of their previous twenty games and looked well on their way to a third straight double-digit-loss record. Many figured this would be the week the defending champions woke up and got rolling—much as they'd done in their only victory of '76: a 31–14 trouncing of the Browns at Three Rivers Stadium in Week Two. Appropriately, the visiting Steelers—who had beaten the Browns five straight times by a combined score of 150–69—were eleven-point favorites.

Things unfolded true to form in the early going on a dreary, rainy afternoon on the lakefront. The Steelers held a 10–6 lead in the second quarter when Brian Sipe was knocked out of the game with a concussion. He wouldn't return and spent the night at Shaker Medical Center. With Mike Phipps lost for the season on opening day, Sipe's replacement was unknown third-stringer Dave Mays, a twenty-seven-year-old rookie who played one year in the World Football League before taking 1975 off to earn his dental degree. Former Browns head coach Blanton Collier, now Cleveland's quarterbacks coach, took Mays—one of the league's first black quarterbacks—under his wing and eased him through the storm. "He told me to block out the crowd, to block out everything going on," Mays said. "It was a crucial game for us as well as them."

Mays avoided the mistakes usually suffered against the Steel Curtain and kept the Browns close, then sparked a turnaround in the third quarter. The Steelers blocked a 51-yard field-goal attempt by Don Cockroft, but since Pittsburgh hadn't made contact until after the ball was past the line of scrimmage, the Browns retained possession after Doug Dieken recovered the loose ball. Moments later, a 29-yard halfback pass from Greg Pruitt to Paul Warfield—re-acquired in the off-season after the infamous 1970 trade with Miami that netted Phipps—set up the go-ahead touchdown: a one-yard plunge by Cleo Miller that made it 12–10, Cleveland. But the play of the day (and perhaps of the decade) would be provided by the Cleveland defense.

Defensive end Joe "Turkey" Jones was already enjoying the finest game of his career when he broke through the Pittsburgh line and targeted quarterback Terry Bradshaw. He reached the wily southern caricature and wrapped him up for what would be the Browns' fourth sack of the day. Jones lifted him into the air and flung him to the ground upside-down, later claiming he couldn't hear referee Bernie Ulman's whistle. Bradshaw landed squarely on his head; his body went limp and his legs twitched reflexively. Though it was a truly terrifying sight, the sellout crowd roared. The Steelers might be in the middle of a never-before-seen run of dominance, but in that moment, the Browns were bigger, stronger, and more intimidating.

Bradshaw would not return, having bruised his spinal column on what would prove to be one of the most controversial plays in the history of the Browns-Steelers rivalry. Though Jones was penalized for unnecessary roughness, several Cleveland players and even writers felt the call was unjust. Even most of the Steelers, including coach Chuck Noll, didn't think Jones intentionally tried to hurt their quarterback. "I saw Turkey drop him on his head," said Steelers center Mike Webster. "Turkey made a helluva play. I can't fault the guy."

Still, the heart and soul of the Steelers—running back Franco Harris and linebacker Jack Lambert—felt differently. "You take somebody and smash them upside down on the ground as hard as you can. That's not trying to hurt somebody?" the intense Lambert asked rhetorically, his voice cracking with emotion. The debate rages to this day. But perhaps the resolution rests in Jones's visit to Bradshaw after the game. The two talked, and the Steelers quarterback forgave the Browns lineman.

With the Stadium crowd now whipped into a frenzy, Cockroft added the game-clinching field goal with under two minutes to play, stretching the Browns' lead to 18–10. After Pittsburgh added a last-minute touchdown, the Browns successfully melted the final seconds for one of the most satisfying victories in team history. With both teams' backs against the wall, the Browns had physically punished the toughest team in football. "The Browns just knocked the hell out of us in the second half," Chuck Noll explained afterward. "It's as simple as that."

It turned out to be the turning point of the season for both squads. For the Browns, the victory was the beginning of a string of eight wins in nine weeks, thrusting them into playoff contention in the greatest one-season turnaround in franchise history. Similarly, after dropping to 1–4, the Steelers ripped off nine straight wins to capture a third straight division title and then cruised to the AFC Championship Game.

Two more Super Bowl titles would follow for the denizens of the Steel City in the next three years, while the Browns would fail to even qualify for the playoffs. Though Pittsburgh's legendary success made the 1970s doubly frustrating for Browns fans, the image of Turkey Jones body slamming Terry Bradshaw that sparked an upset win over the mighty Steelers stirred a sense of pride the city of Cleveland desperately needed in the middle of the darkest decade in civic and athletic history.

	1	2	3	4	
Steelers	7	3	0	6	=16
Browns	3	3	9	3	=18

First Quarter
   CLE-Cockroft 43-yd. FG
   PIT-Harris 1-yd. run (Gerela kick)
Second Quarter
   CLE-Cockroft 28-yd. FG
   PIT-Gerela 30-yd. FG
Third Quarter
   CLE-Miller 1-yd. run (kick failed)
   CLE-Cockroft 50-yd. FG
Fourth Quarter
   CLE-Cockroft 40-yd. FG
   PIT-Kruczek 22-yd. run (kick blocked)

Rushing
PIT-Harris 13–39, Kruczek 2–30, Bleier 8–25, Bradshaw 2–17
CLE-Miller 23–57, G. Pruitt 22–76, Mays 3–14

Passing
PIT-Bradshaw 10–18–1–75, Kruczek 3–5–0–59
CLE-Sipe 4–14–0–80, Mays 5–9–0–70, G. Pruitt 1–1–0–29, Cockroft 0–1–0–0

Receiving
PIT-Swann 3–74, Grossman 3–41, Harris 6–13, Lewis 1–6
CLE-Rucker 3–77, G. Pruitt 4–55, Warfield 2–36, Miller 1–8

#28

Shootout in the Sand

The 1989 Browns had endured a sloppy, schizophrenic season on their way to their fourth division title in five years and, appropriately, the Cleveland Stadium turf on which they'd play their divisional playoff was both sloppy and schizophrenic. Stadium groundskeeper David Frey coyly described the field as having a "lack of grass" and not being "perfectly flat."

Ravaged by one of the cruelest Decembers in Cleveland history, the field was essentially nothing more than a sandlot by the first weekend in January, when the Buffalo Bills came to town to play for a trip to the AFC Championship. What little grass remained was dead and dusty and painted green along with the rest of the field to give off a better appearance on television. Cleveland defensive lineman Al Baker joked he should take a beach towel and tongs out to the field. But as the players took the field to warm up, they knew the condition of the field was no laughing matter.

The streaky Browns had endured a pair of long winless streaks during a wild regular season, symbolized by the bizarre fashion in which they'd clinched the division in Houston two weeks earlier. With victory in their grasp, they'd almost thrown it away when linebacker Clay Matthews decided to lateral after recovering a tide-turning fumble in the final minutes. Much of the sellout crowd could only wonder which Browns squad would show up. Fittingly, both did.

Though the field was miserable, the weather was downright balmy, with the temperature climbing into the mid-thirties, and both offenses came out hot. The Bills, about to embark on an unparalleled run of AFC dominance, drew first blood when quarterback Jim Kelly hit wideout Andre Reed for a 72-yard scoring pass. The Browns responded with a field goal and then took the lead with a bomb of their own when Bernie Kosar connected with Webster Slaughter on a

52-yard strike. After Buffalo crept to a 14–10 lead on another Kelly scoring pass, the Browns surged ahead on a short Kosar–to–Ron Middleton touchdown toss just before the half.

But things wouldn't really get interesting until the second half. Two huge plays in the third quarter gave the Browns control of the contest—another long touchdown toss to Slaughter, then a 90-yard kickoff return for a touchdown by rookie Eric Metcalf. But each time the Browns built a ten-point lead, Buffalo responded with a score of its own. Finally, when Matt Bahr connected on a 47-yard field goal with 6:50 remaining to put Cleveland up 34–24, the hometown crowd began to relax, tasting victory. Though Bud Carson's attack defense had struggled most of the day, the fans were confident the unit would be able to close out the victory and send the Browns to within a step of the Super Bowl.

Instead, with the game on the line, the Cleveland defense evaporated. Time and again, Kelly fired off dump passes to Thurman Thomas, and the versatile running back turned them into substantial gains. With the crowd booing the Browns' inability to adapt, Thomas caught his sixth reception of the drive for a 3-yard touchdown to narrow the margin to 34–30 with 3:56 to play. But Scott Norwood slipped on the treacherous field on the ensuing extra point, and the kick sailed into his offensive line. It would prove to be the difference in the game.

The Browns offense went three-and-out, and Buffalo regained possession at its own twenty-six yard line with 2:41 remaining. With visions of John Elway's 98-yard drive to end the Browns' Super Bowl dreams of three years before floating in front of the fans like a phantom, Kelly picked up where he left off. He marched the Bills to the Cleveland eleven, twice converting on do-or-die fourth-down passes. "I've got to admit," Browns cornerback Hanford Dixon confessed later, "during those final plays, 'The Drive' crossed my mind." With fourteen seconds left, Kelly fired a pass into the end zone that bounced off the hands of wide-open Ronnie Harmon and fell incomplete. The trap door on the scaffold had failed to open, and the Browns were given a second chance with nine seconds showing on the clock.

On the next play, Kelly tried to once again thread the needle to Thomas, who had already caught thirteen passes for a whopping 150 yards. But this time, Thomas was well covered by Clay Matthews, who intercepted the pass at the one yard line and—as he should have done two weeks earlier—fell immediately to the ground, clinching victory.

Two teams from Rust-Belt cities had put up downright glitzy offensive numbers, combining for 778 total yards and forty-two first downs. "It was one of those crazy, wild football games you get in about once every three years," Carson said afterward.

And in its own spunky way, it was one of the most exciting playoff games in Browns history.

	1	2	3	4	
Bills	7	7	7	9	=30
Browns	3	14	14	3	=34

First Quarter
    BUF-Reed 72-yd. pass from Kelly (Norwood kick)
    CLE-Bahr 45-yd. FG
Second Quarter
    CLE-Slaughter 52-yd. pass from Kosar (Bahr kick)
    BUF-Lofton 33-yd. pass from Kelly (Norwood kick)
    CLE-Middleton 3-yd. pass from Kosar (Bahr kick)
Third Quarter
    CLE-Slaughter 44-yd. pass from Kosar (Bahr kick)
    BUF-Thomas 6-yd. pass from Kelly (Norwood kick)
    CLE-Metcalf 90-yd. kickoff return (Bahr kick)
Fourth Quarter
    BUF-Norwood 30-yd. FG
    CLE-Bahr 47-yd. FG
    BUF-Thomas 3-yd. pass from Kelly (kick failed)

RUSHING
BUF-Thomas 10–27, Kinnebrew 7–17, Kelly 1–5
CLE-Mack 12–62, Redden 6–13, Tillman 1–8, Manoa 3–6, Metcalf 4–2, Langhorne 1–0, Kosar 3–(-1)

PASSING
BUF-Kelly 28–54–2–405
CLE-Kosar 20–29–0–251

RECEIVING
BUF-Thomas 13–150, Reed 6–115, Lofton 3–66, Harmon 4–50, Bebee 1–17, Kinnebrew 1–7
CLE-Slaughter 3–114, Langhorne 6–48, Newsome 4–35, Mack 2–19, Brennan 1–15, Middleton 3–12, Metcalf 1–8

seasons when they'd been colleagues in the 1950s, thought the Jets would be the toughest team the Browns would face all season.

Whether or not the rest of America would tune in to watch Keith Jackson, Don Meredith, and Howard Cosell broadcast the first-ever edition of *Monday Night Football,* Cleveland was on board. The largest crowd to ever attend a football game in Cleveland filed through the turnstiles that muggy night: a whopping 85,703. Ironically, despite the record-setting attendance, the historic telecast would be blacked out in Cleveland since the game didn't officially sell out until Monday afternoon.

The Browns scored on their first two possessions, surging to a 14–0 lead, and it appeared they might simply overwhelm Broadway Joe. Instead, Namath caught fire, dissecting the Cleveland defense for the remainder of the night while moving the New York offense up and down the field at will. The Jets cut the margin in half on a short touchdown run by Emerson Boozer, then threatened to score again when they reached the Cleveland seventeen yard line just before intermission. But Browns cornerback Walt Sumner ended the threat when he intercepted Namath. It was the first critical mistake by the Jets on a night overflowing with miscues.

The turning point came on the opening kickoff of the second half. New Browns wideout Homer Jones—acquired from the Giants to help fill the void left after the trade of Paul Warfield—returned the boot ninety-four yards for a touchdown and a 21–7 advantage. Though the Jets would dominate Cleveland for the rest of the night, more than doubling the home team in total yardage (455 to 221), the Browns never lost control of the game, thanks to four Jet turnovers and a whopping 161 yards in New York penalties. When New York cut the margin to seven, Don Cockroft pushed it back up to ten. When the Jets picked up a first down at the Cleveland seven yard line early in the fourth quarter, running back Matt Snell fumbled, and Browns defensive end Jack Gregory recovered. Cleveland linebacker Jim Houston halted another drive with an interception.

Yet, just when the Browns appeared poised to put the game out of reach, they let New York wiggle off the hook. Cockroft missed an 18-yard field goal that could have put the Browns up by thirteen, and Namath responded, driving his club eighty yards in just four plays and cutting the margin to 24–21 with a 33-yard scoring pass to George Sauer. When the Browns couldn't run out the clock with their next possession, the stage was set for Namath to be the hero once again.

The Browns caught a break when New York's Mike Battle misjudged Cockroft's ensuing punt and let it bounce at the New York thirty. It rolled all the way to the four, where the Jets took over with 1:30 to play. Namath picked up a first down at the Jets eighteen with a minute left then tried to force a pass over the middle. Cleveland linebacker Billy Andrews—who'd just entered the game to spell Dale Lindsey—picked off the toss for his first career interception, spilled to the ground, then got up and rumbled twenty-five yards to the end zone for the game-clinching touchdown.

The game had marked more than just the beginning of a fresh season for the Browns and a bold new decade for the league. With the successful debut of *Monday Night Football,* the NFL was about to demand a new position in the American consciousness.

	1	2	3	4	
Jets	0	7	7	7	=21
Browns	14	0	10	7	=31

First Quarter
   CLE-Collins 8-yd. pass from Nelsen (Cockroft kick)
   CLE-Scott 2-yd. run (Cockroft kick)
Second Quarter
   NY-Boozer 2-yd. run (Turner kick)
Third Quarter
   CLE-Jones 94-yd. kickoff return (Cockroft kick)
   NY-Boozer 10-yd. run (Turner kick)
   CLE-Cockroft 27-yd. FG
Fourth Quarter
   NY-Sauer 33-yd. pass from Namath (Turner kick)
   CLE-Andrews 25-yd. INT return (Cockroft kick)

RUSHING
NY-Snell 17–108, Boozer 14–58, Nock 1–3, White 1–0
CLE-Kelly 20–62, Scott 9–12, Nelsen 1–2

PASSING
NY-Namath 19–32–3–284, Woodall 1–2–0–7
CLE-Nelsen 12–27–0–145

RECEIVING
NY-Sauer 10–172, Maynard 4–69, Boozer 3–38, Caster 1–19, Stewart 1–7, White 1–1
CLE-Morin 5–90, Scott 4–21, Collins 2–21, Hooker 1–13

#26

BROWNS 26, CINCINNATI BENGALS 10
DECEMBER 17, 1995

The End

It was the most bizarre day in the history of Cleveland sports.

The atmosphere surrounding Cleveland Stadium on this sunny, crisp December afternoon was surreal, like something out of a Ray Bradbury story. Thousands of fans trudged slowly toward the old ballpark on the lake without an ounce of enthusiasm, most driven only by a combination of rage, nostalgia, and confusion.

It seemed like a generation had passed since both *Sports Illustrated* and *The Sporting News* picked the 1995 Browns to reach the Super Bowl less than four months before. It had been six weeks since Art Modell had stood on the Baltimore waterfront and officially announced he was moving the Browns to Maryland—a day that sent the city of Cleveland spiraling into a tempest of emotion. Petitions were signed, rallies were held, court orders were filed. The news spread around the globe, and the entire sports world focused its attention on victimized Cleveland, Ohio, and its long-suffering fans who refused to accept this injustice. NBC's Bob Costas lambasted Modell on the air, calling the potential move "one of the outrages of the century in the world of sports." Perhaps even worse, the league claimed it was powerless to stop it. "The NFL would have thrown Cleveland out like leftovers from last week except for the eruption of protests in this city," Bill Livingston wrote.

But after six weeks and six straight Browns losses, confusion still reigned. Modell's cabal had opened offices in Baltimore the first week in December, but no one really knew for sure if the Browns' Week Sixteen encounter with Cincinnati would be the team's final game ever in Cleveland. Would the city prevail in its legal battle and keep the Browns? Even that scenario was muddy;

there was the possibility Modell could successfully move the team, and it would practice in Baltimore but still play its games in Cleveland.

And if the Browns did move, there were no guarantees that Cleveland would get another team. Landing a brand-new expansion team looked slim—more likely was the possibility of another NFL franchise moving to Cleveland, perhaps the Houston Oilers or Tampa Bay Buccaneers or, ironically, the rival Bengals, whom the Browns would close the 1995 home schedule against. Even more interestingly, the Baltimore posse which had wooed Modell had reportedly offered the same deal to Cincinnati owner Mike Brown to move his Bengals to Baltimore, but he turned it down.

The national media swooped into Cleveland as if the Browns were hosting a conference championship. For the first time ever in the regular season, NBC hosted its pre-game show from Cleveland. The 55,000-plus fans who attended the game would have their tickets stamped, not torn, in case they did become commemorative souvenirs. When the fans settled into the tomb-like stands, even the familiar backdrop of the Stadium was tainted—every advertisement banner had been removed as local and national companies pulled their agreements. In their place, team officials had hung preposterous "Thank You Art" banners, though Modell would not attend the game or even return to his Waite Hill home, under the threat of death.

At the request of the players, individual pre-game introductions were nixed. If possible, the players were even more confused than the fans. They'd never been told of the move before it was reported by the media and had no idea where or even if they'd be employed in another month. Still, most felt obligated to acknowledge the fans and the city in some way. "I hope each of us can do something special for the fans to remember us and for us to remember them," Vinny Testaverde said. "It's a special day, a sad day. . . . I just think that individually, it would be nice for the players to thank the fans in their own way."

That's exactly what the Browns did: Playing solely out of respect for the fans who had stood by them for so long, the Browns dominated the Cincinnati Bengals, roaring to a 17–3 halftime lead and putting the game away in the second half. Testaverde played one of his finest games, completing twenty-two of thirty-two passes for 241 yards and a pair of touchdowns as the previously anemic Cleveland offense rolled up 400 total yards. But what was actually taking place on the field seemed secondary. As Mike Brown said later, "the event outweighed the game."

Originally the team had planned a tribute to great running backs of the Browns' past during the game, but the event had obviously been cancelled.

Instead, veteran Earnest Byner put on a show all by himself. Used sparingly since returning to Cleveland the year before, Byner put forth perhaps his finest effort in a Browns uniform, rushing for 121 yards and catching seven passes. Byner touched the football on thirty-eight of the Browns' seventy-three plays from scrimmage. He would receive a game ball and had it signed by Jim Brown in the locker room.

As the final minutes ticked off the clock, what little sanity remained in the Stadium snapped. Fans in the Dog Pound began ripping the bleachers from the stands and tossing them onto the field in symbolic protest, causing the officials to make the teams switch ends of the field midway through the fourth quarter. Firecrackers went off in the stands, echoing through the Stadium like gunshots. The chants of "Modell Sucks" became so loud that "Jingle Bell Rock" was blasted over the PA system to drown them out. When the clock finally hit zero, a handful of Browns were drawn to the Pound, where they hugged and high-fived fans, many of whom were sobbing. "People didn't want to let you go," Byner said. "They wanted to hold your hand. They'd shake your hand and then grab it with both of their hands, and you almost had to pull them out of the stands to get your hand back." All sense of time and place seemed to melt away. "It seemed like five minutes," Browns center Steve Everitt said, "but I think we were actually out there close to an hour."

High above the field, Browns play-by-play announcer Casey Coleman broke down on the air. Longtime Browns tackle Tony Jones knelt at midfield for a long time, soaking in the emotion. "I didn't want this day to be over," he said later.

But eventually, it ended. And when it did, the Cleveland Browns were no more.

	1	2	3	4	
Bengals	0	3	0	7	=10
Browns	0	17	6	3	=26

Second Quarter
   CLE-Hartley 1-yd. pass from Testaverde (Stover kick)
   CIN-Pelfrey 30-yd. FG
   CLE-Stover 37-yd. FG
   CLE-McCardell 16-yd. pass from Testaverde (Stover kick)
Third Quarter
   CLE-Stover 42-yd. FG
   CLE-Stover 19-yd. FG

Fourth Quarter
  CLE-Stover 35-yd. FG
  CIN-Bieniemy 1-yd. run (Pelfrey kick)

RUSHING
CIN-Green 7–33, Bieniemy 5–18, Blake 4–14
CLE-Byner 31–121, Powers 9–29, Testaverde 1–9

PASSING
CIN-Blake 22–46–1–257
CLE-Testaverde 22–32–0–241

RECEIVING
CIN-Pickens 5–90, McGee 2–43, Scott 4–36, Dunn 4–30, Hill 1–18, Green
  2–17, Joseph 3–14, Bieniemy 1–9
CLE-Rison 6–73, Jackson 3–61, Byner 7–36, McCardell 3–33, Hartley 2–21,
  Bishop 1–17

BROWNS 31, CINCINNATI BENGALS 27
DECEMBER 5, 1971

Central Showdown

In their first year in the NFL, the Cincinnati Bengals had pulled off one of the most remarkable turnarounds in the history of football. After limping to a 1–6 start, the 1970 Bengals won seven in a row to capture their first winning record along with the first-ever AFC Central Division title. And the game that turned Cincy's season around was a 14–10 victory over the Browns at Riverfront Stadium, which turned out to comprise the one-game difference between the teams in the final standings.

Now, with the 1971 season winding to its conclusion, the Bengals were trying their best to recreate their improbable magic from the year before. This time Cincy slipped to 1–7 before turning things around, winning three straight to pull within two games of front-running Cleveland with three games to play. If the Bengals could win their Week Twelve showdown with the Browns at cold and muddy Cleveland Stadium, they'd be right in the mix for a second straight division title. On the other hand, if the Browns could hold off the Bengals and Pittsburgh lost in Houston, Cleveland would capture its first Central crown. Ironically, the Browns themselves had endured an up-and-down year, sprinting to a 4–1 record then losing four straight before righting the ship. The stage was set for what would go down as one of the most dramatic encounters in the history of the rivalry.

The favored Bengals made a key mistake by fumbling the opening kickoff, which led directly to a Browns touchdown. Yet Cincinnati rebounded and surged to a 20–7 lead late in the second quarter and threatened to blow the contest open. But the momentum swung with five seconds left in the half when Bill Nelsen hit streaking wideout Fair Hooker for a 39-yard touchdown pass across the middle to cut the lead to six. The Browns then took the lead in the third quarter when Nelsen fired a deep pass for wide receiver Frank Pitts. Cincy corner Lemar Parrish leapt for the ball and appeared to have it, but Pitts ripped it from Parrish and ran the remaining twenty yards to complete a 53-yard touchdown pass to the delight of the capacity crowd of 82,705.

The Bengals responded as running back Essex Johnson broke free for an 86-yard touchdown run early in the fourth quarter that put Cincy back ahead 27–21. After a 35-yard run by Bo Scott, the Browns cut the margin to three with a short Don Cockroft field goal, then, with time running out, regained possession at their own twenty and began marching. Twice Nelsen came through with key third-down completions, and veteran tailback Leroy Kelly rose to the occasion, touching the ball five times on the drive. His fourth touch was an 18-yard run to the Cincinnati four yard line.

On the next play, Kelly, coming to the end of a legendary career, took a handoff on a sweep and, following a block from Gene Hickerson, carved through the Cincinnati defense as he'd done all day. Wrapped up by linebacker Bill Bergey at the one yard line, Kelly stretched the ball over the goal line for the go-ahead touchdown with 1:48 to play.

Moments later, an Ernie Kellerman interception halted Cincinnati's final drive and clinched the game. As news filtered into the Stadium that the Steelers had been pounded in Houston, Cleveland fans rushed the field as the clock hit zero, celebrating the team's first division championship and, as Hal Lebovitz wrote, "one of the finest spectator games ever played" in Cleveland.

	1	2	3	4	
Bengals	10	10	0	7	=27
Browns	7	7	7	10	=31

First Quarter
  CLE-Kelly 1-yd. run (Cockroft kick)
  CIN-Muhlmann 46-yd. FG
  CIN-Dressler 4-yd. run (Muhlmann kick)
Second Quarter
  CIN-Willis 9-yd. run (Muhlmann kick)
  CIN-Muhlmann 24-yd. FG
  CLE-Hooker 39-yd. pass from Nelsen (Cockroft kick)
Third Quarter
  CLE-Pitts 53-yd. pass from Nelsen (Cockroft kick)
Fourth Quarter
  CIN-Johnson 86-yd. run (Muhlmann kick)

CLE-Cockroft 12-yd. FG
CLE-Kelly 4-yd. run (Cockroft kick)

Rushing
CIN-Johnson 4–109, Willis 17–79, Dressler 12–39, Carter 1–5
CLE-Kelly 23–127, Scott 12–61, Nelsen 3–(-6)

Passing
CIN-Carter 13–23–1–118
CLE-Nelsen 14–28–2–224

Receiving
CIN-Trumpy 3–43, Dressler 6–26, Myers 3–26, Johnson 1–23
CLE-Pitts 5–103, Hooker 5–80, Morin 3–35, Scott 1–6

#24

MIAMI DOLPHINS 20, BROWNS 14
DECEMBER 24, 1972

A Christmas Eve Reprieve

The 1972 Miami Dolphins had a date with destiny, and it seemed nobody could prevent it. Certainly not the Cleveland Browns, who had no All-Pro players, hadn't even won their division, and only qualified for the playoffs as a Wild Card team.

The Dolphins, with a whopping nine Pro Bowl selections, were on the brink of history. They'd become the first team in modern NFL history to complete the regular season undefeated and were now just three victories away from a perfect season. Along the way, Miami set a league record with 2,951 team rushing yards and became the first team to have two players run for a thousand yards in a season—Larry Csonka and Mercury Morris. Even more painful for Browns backers, Miami's passing game was based around wideout Paul Warfield, whom the Browns had traded two years earlier. Miami, thirteen-point favorites, would host the upstarts on Christmas Eve afternoon at the Orange Bowl, where the Dolphins had won thirteen straight games.

Since nobody gave the Browns a chance, they figured they had nothing to lose. "They have won fourteen in a row, but now everything is even," said Browns center Bob DeMarco, who had played for Miami the previous season. "Now the money games are here. It seems to me the pressure is on them."

"Get a rat in a corner," coach Nick Skorich said, "and he fights for his life." Hal Lebovitz opined, "Wouldn't it be a great Christmas present to fans here if they could score an upset? It would be as big a reversal as the one Joe Namath and the Jets pulled in the . . . Super Bowl."

Plus, the tone for a wild weekend of playoff football was set Saturday with a pair of the most incredible finishes in NFL history. The Steelers triumphed over Oakland thanks to Franco Harris's "Immaculate Reception" while Roger

Staubach played "Captain Comeback" for the first time, bringing Dallas back from a fifteen-point fourth-quarter deficit to beat the 49ers. Could the zaniness carry over to Sunday?

Early on, it appeared not. Mike Phipps's first pass was intercepted, setting the tone for one of the worst days of his fledgling career. Though Cleveland dodged a bullet when Garo Yepremian missed a field goal, minutes later, an early gamble paid off for the Dolphins when Charley Babb blocked a Don Cockroft punt and then returned it five yards for the game's first touchdown. The Browns were poised to tie the game when a 25-yard Phipps scramble set them up at the Miami twenty-five yard line late in the first quarter, but Frank Pitts dropped a sure touchdown pass, then Curtis Johnson picked off Phipps moments later, ending the threat. The lead swelled to 10–0, and it appeared the Dolphins were off to the races.

But the Browns hung tough. While the offense struggled to ignite facing Miami's talented "No-Name Defense," Cleveland's defenders contained the Dolphins' heralded running attack. Still down ten in the third quarter, Cleveland finally put points on the board when Phipps scrambled around right end for a five-yard touchdown run. After the Dolphins stretched the margin to 13–7, the Browns responded again with a lengthy drive. Once again it seemed they would come away empty when Phipps was intercepted by defensive back Dick Anderson, but Anderson fumbled the football on the return, and Browns wideout Fair Hooker recovered, giving the Browns new life. Appropriately, two plays later Hooker reeled in a 27-yard touchdown pass to give the Browns a 14–13 lead. They were now eight minutes away from the biggest upset in NFL history.

But the Dolphins offense, which had been held in check all day, finally got rolling. Quarterback Earl Morrall directed Miami on an 80-yard march capped by an eight-yard touchdown run by Jim Kiick to put the Dolphins back up by six with four minutes left. After being forced to punt, the Browns had one final chance. They drove to the Miami thirty-four yard line before Phipps was picked off for the fifth time, securing a Miami victory and ending the Dolphins' biggest scare of the season. Accordingly, there was little celebration in the Miami locker room. "They seemed like men who had just received a reprieve from the governor while on the way to execution," Chuck Heaton wrote.

Meanwhile, in the Cleveland locker room, Skorich implored his players to keep their heads up. They'd just given one of the greatest teams in the history of football their toughest game. Their effort was appreciated back in Cleveland as well. "The Browns can join their families and open those Christmas presents today with heads held high," wrote Heaton. "They didn't pull off that hoped-for miracle, but they came close enough to gain new respect in the National Football League and make the future of the club seem bright."

The box score demanded that respect. The Browns had outplayed the mighty Dolphins in several phases. Csonka was held to thirty-two yards on fourteen carries, and Miami was nearly twenty yards below their per-game rushing average. Warfield only caught two passes, and with Cleveland tackles Walter Johnson and Jerry Sherk leading a ferocious pass rush, Morrall was sacked four times. Most notably, the Browns out-gained the Dolphins in total yardage. But Phipps's five interceptions were too much to overcome.

"Possibly at no time in their history," Dan Coughlin wrote, "have the Browns proved so much to each other and to their detractors despite defeat."

Three weeks later, the 1972 Miami Dolphins did indeed certify their legacy, comfortably winning Super Bowl VII and completing a 17–0 season that may never be matched. But their near-brush with disaster against the Browns is frozen as a footnote to history.

	1	2	3	4	
Browns	0	0	7	7	=14
Dolphins	10	0	0	10	=20

First Quarter
   MIA-Babb 5-yd. blocked punt return (Yepremian kick)
   MIA-Yepremian 40-yd. FG
Third Quarter
   CLE-Phipps 5-yd. run (Cockroft kick)
Fourth Quarter
   MIA-Yepremian 46-yd. FG
   CLE-Hooker 27-yd. pass from Phipps (Cockroft kick)
   MIA-Kiick 8-yd. run (Yepremian kick)

RUSHING
CLE-Scott 16–94, Phipps 8–47, Brown 4–13, Kelly 4–11
MIA-Morris 15–72, Kiick 14–50, Warfield 2–41, Csonka 14–32, Morrall 4–3

PASSING
CLE-Phipps 9–23–5–131
MIA-Morrall 6–13–0–88

RECEIVING

CLE-Hooker 3–53, Scott 4–30, Kelly 1–27, Morin 1–21
MIA-Twilley 3–33, Warfield 2–30, Kiick 1–5

#23

BROWNS 21, NEW ORLEANS SAINTS 16
OCTOBER 31, 1999

Full of Grace

"War is hell," former Cleveland Cavaliers coach Bill Fitch said during the team's pitiful inaugural season in 1970. "Expansion is worse."

Twenty-nine years later, Cleveland sports fans were reminded of the painful truth of that statement. The initial warm glow of the Browns' triumphant return to the NFL had long since worn off and now fans were wondering if the '99 Browns would actually win a game. After being clobbered by Pittsburgh in the opener, the expansion Browns went on to drop their next six contests. Rookie wide receiver Kevin Johnson had tried to shake things up the week before, guaranteeing a victory over the 5–0 St. Louis Rams, but the Browns were throttled, 34–3.

After blowing a golden opportunity to win a game over Cincinnati in Week Five and the most difficult portion of the schedule still ahead, an 0–16 record began to look like a very real possibility. Even worse, some felt the expansion Tampa Bay Buccaneers' string of ineptitude that became a league-record twenty-six-game losing streak two decades earlier was also in danger of falling, particularly if the Browns couldn't somehow defeat the 1–5 New Orleans Saints on Halloween afternoon in the Louisiana Superdome—where the Bucs' losing streak had come to an end in 1977.

Despite losing five straight themselves, the Saints were ten-point favorites and would try to ride rookie running back Ricky Williams to victory. A week after racking up the first 100-yard game of his career, Williams would carry the ball forty times and roll over the Browns for a whopping 179 yards. But he would also cough up three key fumbles, thus opening the door for the Browns. New Orleans established itself as the better team early, but the Browns stayed close. Making his seventh professional start, Tim Couch played the finest game of his young career, tossing a pair of long touchdown passes. The second, a 25-yard toss to Johnson, gave Cleveland a 14–10 lead midway through the third quarter, and fans back in Cleveland began to believe this could be the day.

But the Saints rallied, cutting the lead to one going into the fourth period. After Browns kicker Phil Dawson missed a critical 47-yard field goal, the Saints put together a clutch drive in the final minutes. They appeared to clinch victory with a 46-yard field goal by Doug Brien with twenty-one seconds on the clock to make it 16–14. The Browns, by all appearances, had blown another great chance.

Yet New Orleans had left the door open just a crack. Rather than running the clock down and letting the field goal be the last play of the game, Saints quarterback Billy Joe Tolliver had called his final time-out too early, allowing the Browns one final possession. As the members of the offense gathered around their beleaguered, battered rookie leader in the huddle, Couch looked in their eyes and said, "We're going to get this one." Couch dropped back from the Cleveland twenty-five yard line and connected with wideout Leslie Shepherd for a 19-yard gain at the forty-four. Shepherd quickly toppled out of bounds to stop the clock with two seconds left.

The final play of the game was called "258 Flood Tip Right." Darrin Chiaverini, Shepherd, and Johnson all lined up on the right side and streaked toward the end zone. As Johnson motored downfield, he looked up at the giant television screen hanging from the Superdome rafters, where he saw Saints defensive end Brady Smith explode past Cleveland left tackle Lomas Brown on the left side of the Browns line and close in on Couch. The play would have been busted from that moment but luckily was designed for Couch to roll to his right, away from Smith.

Just before he reached the sideline and with the clock showing double-zeroes, Couch stopped and heaved the football high into the air, "as long and as high as I could," he said later. Seven players—three Browns and four Saints—gathered in the end zone as the Hail Mary pass floated down. Following the play just as it was drawn up, Shepherd settled in the middle of the gathering pack in the end zone to serve as the "tipper." As Chiaverini and Johnson formed a halo around him, New Orleans defensive backs Tyronne Drakeford and Sammy Knight leapt into the air to prevent Shepherd from catching the pass. The football was deflected, and it caromed right into the arms of Kevin Johnson, who squeezed the ball to his chest and looked down to see his two white shoes in stark contrast against the black paint of the end zone. He fell to the ground and looked up to see the side judge carefully hold up both arms. "I saw the referee raise his arms real slow," Couch said, "like he didn't believe it either."

But it had happened, and nobody could quite believe it. Knight put it best: "That play happens once a millennium."

For one bizarre moment, Browns players and coaches simply looked at one another in stunned disbelief. "Just to see all of our reactions after he caught the ball is going to be something we can all remember for a long time," Couch said. Then reality hit home. The players, led by Couch, sprinted to the end zone and piled on top of one another in childlike glee. "If there was no roof covering the Louisiana Superdome, you'd swear the first victory for the new Browns was dropped from a place far, far above," Tony Grossi wrote. "Winning this way was way bigger than any of us," said tight end Irv Smith. "You could not have written a script like this and have it make any sense."

Indeed not. For after 1,409 days, the Cleveland Browns had finally won a football game—in the most dramatic fashion imaginable.

	1	2	3	4	
Browns	0	7	7	7	=21
Saints	7	3	3	3	=16

First Quarter
NO-Poole 5-yd. pass from Hobert (Brien kick)
Second Quarter
CLE-Edwards 27-yd. pass from Couch (Dawson kick)
NO-Brien 49-yd. FG
Third Quarter
CLE-Johnson 24-yd. pass from Couch
NO-Brien 22-yd. FG
Fourth Quarter
NO-Brien 46-yd. FG
CLE-Johnson 56-yd. pass from Couch (Dawson kick)

RUSHING
CLE-Abdul-Jabbar 13–39, Kirby 6–18, Couch 2–5
NO-Williams 40–179, Tolliver 4–24, Smith 4–17, Hobert 1–9, Craver 1–2

PASSING
CLE-Couch 11–19–0–193
NO-Tolliver 9–20–1–92, Hobert 4–9–1–28

RECEIVING

CLE-Johnson 4–96, Shepherd 4–52, Edwards 2–37, Kirby 1–8

NO-Craver 2–32, Kennison 2–27, Poole 3–23, Dawsey 1–11, Smith 1–11, Williams 3–8, Cleeland 1–8

#22

NEW YORK GIANTS 13, BROWNS 10
DECEMBER 14, 1958

The Phantom Fumble

Though there was still a week to go in the regular season, Cleveland sports fans had already turned their attention to the 1958 NFL Championship. The media was hyping the upcoming showdown between the Browns and Baltimore Colts and trying to determine which team would have the upper hand.

And with good reason. The Browns were in perfect position to clinch their eighth Eastern Conference title in nine years—all it would take was either a win or a tie in the regular-season finale against the Giants in New York. Even if the Giants won, it would set up a playoff between the teams a week later. Since New York had barely slipped past the Browns earlier in the season, nobody could see the Giants beating Cleveland two more times in successive weeks. And though the Browns and Giants had similar records going into the finale (9–2 and 8–3), the consensus was that Cleveland had faced a much tougher schedule. Anything could happen, Gordon Cobbledick admitted in the *Plain Dealer,* "but it is reasonable to assume that they are too formidable to lose three times to a team that has been beaten by such as the Eagles, the Cardinals and the Steelers." Even New York coach Jim Lee Howell rode the wave of public opinion. "They look like a cinch to win the division title, don't they?" he said, only half-kidding.

After sixteen inches of snow buried the Cleveland area the week before, the Browns were eager to get out of town. They'd left the sub-zero temperatures back in Cleveland, but the snow followed them and wound up providing a Christmas-card setting for the game. Even with the elements a factor, Cobbledick wasn't concerned. "This department assures you this morning," he wrote in Sunday's *Plain Dealer,* "that by nightfall the Cleveland Browns will be reigning champions of the National Professional Football League's Eastern division."

Cobbledick's confidence seemed prophetic on the game's first play when Jim Brown exploded through the line on a play just added to the game plan the previous week and sprinted sixty-five yards for a touchdown—his eighteenth of the season, tying the NFL record. With Brown on the way to a dazzling 158-yard performance, it appeared the tone had been set. Then quarterback Milt Plum hit Ray Renfro for a 51-yard gain in the second quarter that set up a Lou Groza field goal. With snow falling steadily and resourceful fans building small bonfires in the Yankee Stadium bleachers, the Browns dominated the contest through three quarters. Yet they missed several chances to pull away. An early Lew Carpenter fumble led to New York's only points of the first half, while Lou Groza missed two short field goals. Then, after a dominant twelve-minute drive to start the third quarter, Paul Brown called for a peculiar fake field goal on a chip-shot 30-yard attempt on fourth-and-eight that backfired miserably. Thus, the Browns' lead was just 10–3 going into what would become one of the most memorable fourth quarters in team history.

The tide began to turn when Plum fumbled at midfield, and the Giants recovered. After a 39-yard halfback option pass from Frank Gifford to end Kyle Rote, the opportunistic Giants went to the well once again. They tied the game on another halfback-option pass from Gifford to Bowling Green product Bob Schnelker that just eluded the reach of Cleveland defensive back Ken Konz. The Giants missed a chance to take the lead with five minutes left when kicker Pat Summerall hooked a 33-yard field goal, but the Browns returned the favor by stalling on their next drive. Then Dick DeSchaine's punt went off the side of his foot, traveling only twenty-two yards to the Browns forty-four, putting the Giants in perfect position to collect the winning points.

After quarterback Charley Conerly threw a pair of incompletions, he looped a pass over the middle for Gifford, who appeared to catch it at the thirty yard line, then was blasted by Browns linebacker Galen Fiss. The football popped loose, and Walt Michaels scooped it up and started downfield, apparently punching the Browns' ticket to the NFL title game. That Gifford had fumbled didn't seem to be in doubt. Conerly ripped his helmet off and threw it to the ground, and the New York defensive unit began to downheartedly march onto the field. But for one puzzling second, the officiating crew was paralyzed by confusion. "The officials just stood there," Paul Brown said later. "No one wanted to call the play."

Finally, linesman Charley Barry did. He ruled Gifford never had control of the pass and that it was incomplete. "It was a judgment play," Howell would say later, though most figured it was bad judgment. Either way, it gave the Giants one last chance with just over two minutes remaining. After contemplating whether to send out Summerall for a 49-yard field-goal attempt in the swirling snow or try to pin the Browns in the shadow of their own goal and hope the New York defense could win the game, Howell opted to go for the field goal. Summerall atoned for his earlier miss by launching a rocket through the flurries and into the history books.

The Browns didn't give up, driving into New York territory in the final minute. But after Plum was thrown for an 11-yard loss in the final seconds, Groza's 55-yard field-goal attempt fell short as time expired. The Browns would have to return to New York seven days later for a playoff.

"Look at them," Paul Brown grumbled, motioning toward his shell-shocked players in the locker room afterward. "They still don't believe it. They don't think they lost that football game. . . . There isn't a man in this room who doesn't think that Frank Gifford fumbled that ball."

That disbelief only grew the following week as the Giants defense smothered Jim Brown and the Cleveland offense, and New York coasted to a 10–0 victory to set up a title clash with Johnny Unitas and the Colts—a game considered by many to be the greatest ever played.

	1	2	3	4	
Browns	7	3	0	0	=10
Giants	0	3	0	10	=13

First Quarter
    CLE-Brown 65-yd. run (Groza kick)
Second Quarter
    NY-Summerall 46-yd. FG
    CLE-Groza 23-yd. FG
Fourth Quarter
    NY-Schnelker 7-yd. pass from Gifford (Summerall kick)
    NY-Summerall 49-yd. FG

RUSHING
CLE-Brown 26–158, L. Carpenter 8–9, Plum 3–1
NY-Webster 8–40, Gifford 6–15, King 3–11, Triplett 5–8

PASSING
CLE-Plum 6–12–0–140
NY-Conerly 10–29–0–162, Gifford 2–3–0–46, Heinrich 3–5–0–22

Receiving

CLE-Renfro 2–64, P. Carpenter 2–55, Brewster 1–12, L. Carpenter 1–9
NY-Webster 5–58, Rote 2–48, Gifford 4–35, Shiker 2–20, King 2–9

#21

BROWNS 34, CINCINNATI BENGALS 3
DECEMBER 14, 1986

Who Dey?

For only the fourth time in the seventeen-year history of the AFC Central Division, the first- and second-place teams would square off within the final two weeks of the season with the division title hanging in the balance. "Call it a showdown, call it whatever you want," Marty Schottenheimer said that week. "This is what it's all about."

Yet for all the excitement sparked by their Week Fifteen showdown with the Bengals in Cincinnati, things didn't look all that promising for the Browns. True, at 10–4 they held a one-game lead over the Bengals, but Cincy had throttled the Browns in their previous meeting in Cleveland in September. With another victory, the Bengals, winners of three of their last four and boasting the hottest offense in the NFL, could move into a first-place tie and snag the critical tie-breaker over the Browns. What's more, they'd have a raucous home crowd behind them, chanting the team motto—"Who dey think gonna beat dem Bengals?" On a cold but sunny December afternoon, nearly 60,000 fans packed into Riverfront Stadium, where the Bengals had won ten of their last eleven games and four straight over the Browns.

Hoping to rattle second-year quarterback Bernie Kosar, a Cincinnati radio station handed out thousands of paper megaphones called "Bernie Blasters." And when Kosar and the offense took the field for the first play from scrimmage, those blasters were in full force, creating a volcano of noise that echoed through Riverfront. Kosar calmly took the snap, dropped back, and lofted a long pass down the right sideline for wideout Reggie Langhorne. Langhorne reeled it in at the Cincinnati twenty-seven yard line and coasted down the field before being tripped up at the Bengal one after a 66-yard gain. As suddenly as the crowd had come to life, it hushed. A play later, the Browns took a 7–0 lead, and the rout was on.

The Cincinnati offense was the best in football, averaging 400 total yards per game, and had rolled up nearly 600 in New England the week before. But against the Browns, the Bengals were stymied all afternoon. Quarterback Boomer Esiason threw a pair of interceptions and was beaten to a pulp. "I have never played against a more ferocious pass rush since coming to Cincinnati," Esiason admitted after the game. "It's the most physical game I've played in as a pro." Meanwhile, Kosar and the Cleveland offense quietly ripped the Cincinnati defense to pieces with a near-flawless performance: no turnovers, no sacks. Late in the first quarter, Kosar hooked up with Webster Slaughter for a 47-yard scoring pass, and the lead swelled to 17–3 at the intermission. When Cincinnati failed to convert on a risky fourth-and-six attempt at the Browns twenty-eight on the opening drive of the second half, the air went out of the Bengals' high-flying balloon.

The second half became a clinic as the Browns utterly dominated Cincinnati, landing knockout punch after knockout punch. A Felix Wright interception of Esiason led to another Kevin Mack touchdown, and when Slaughter recovered a Curtis Dickey fumble in the end zone for Cleveland's fourth touchdown four minutes later, the Browns held a commanding 31–3 lead. There was no doubt this day belonged to the Browns. "We kicked their butts," Browns lineman Sam Clancy said. "We showed them and everybody today that we're the best team."

The final was 34–3, as the Browns captured their second straight division title and biggest win ever over the rival Bengals. "It was one small step for a team," Tony Grossi wrote, "one giant leap for a franchise." And in so doing, they'd provided the elusive answer to the "Who dey?" question Bengal fans had presented to anyone who would listen.

	1	2	3	4	
Browns	14	3	14	3	=34
Bengals	3	0	0	0	= 3

First Quarter
   CLE-Mack 1-yd. run (Moseley kick)
   CIN-Breech 22-yd. FG
   CLE-Slaughter 47-yd. pass from Kosar (Moseley kick)
Second Quarter
   CLE-Moseley 39-yd. FG

Third Quarter
  CLE-Mack 1-yd. run (Moseley kick)
  CLE-Slaughter recovers Dickey's fumble in end zone (Moseley kick)
Fourth Quarter
  CLE-Moseley 19-yd. FG

RUSHING
CLE-Mack 23–93, Dickey 13–37, Fontenot 1–3, Kosar 1–(-7)
CIN-Wilson 10–60, Brooks 12–43, Kinnebrew 3–35, McGee 2–2, Jennings
  2–(-2), Brown 1–(-3)

PASSING
CLE-Kosar 13–29–0–246
CIN-Esiason 14–31–2–151, Anderson 1–1–0–17

RECEIVING
CLE-Slaughter 3–75, Langhorne 1–66, Brennan 3–33, Fontenot 2–32, Newsome 2–32, Weathers 1–5, Mack 1–3
CIN-Brooks 7–75, Brown 4–47, Holman 2–21, Kreider 1–17, Collinsworth
  1–8

#20

Salvation in the House of Pain

Never before in Browns history would one game so dramatically define an entire season. If the Browns could upset the Houston Oilers in the Astrodome—nicknamed the "House of Pain" by the resurgent Oilers—two days before Christmas, the roller-coaster 1989 season would go down as an unqualified success. First-year coach Bud Carson would have returned the team to the top of the AFC Central Division after a year's respite despite a handful of aging, injured core players. But if the Browns lost the game, 1989 would be an unmitigated disaster. Cleveland would miss the playoffs for the first time in five years, barely finishing over .500 after failing to win five of its last six games.

The determination would be made during an old-fashioned Saturday-night shootout in snowbound Houston, Texas—a winner-take-all brawl with the division title hanging in the balance.

The Browns, who had won for the first time in a month the prior week, threatened to turn the shootout into an execution. Thanks to a pair of big plays, they surged to a 17–0 second-quarter lead. First, battered Bernie Kosar hit Eric Metcalf on an innocent play over the middle that the rookie from Texas turned into a 68-yard touchdown with a half-dozen athletic jukes and cuts. Then, late in the second quarter from the Houston forty yard line, Kosar flung a bomb for Webster Slaughter (who was enjoying the finest season of his career) and, fighting through good coverage, Slaughter pinned the football against his facemask and held on for a touchdown. In what had been an up-and-down season, the Browns had apparently brought their A-game. But, appropriately, there were a few more dips to come.

The Oilers surged back into the game, cutting the margin to 17–13 early in the fourth quarter. Then, with less than six minutes to play, Houston was marching again with a first down at the Cleveland fifteen when a blown count led to the football being snapped right past quarterback Warren Moon. Clay Matthews recovered for the Browns at the thirty-three yard line, and the visitors appeared to have victory in their grasp. But then Matthews whirled around and, inexplicably, tried to lateral the football to Browns lineman Chris Pike. The ball sailed over Pike's head and hit the turf at the twenty-eight, where Oilers wideout Ernest Givins recovered, giving the Oilers a new set of downs and new life. "When Clay decided to lateral the football," Carson said later, "I began to think it was not meant to be."

On the next play, Houston appeared to put the nail in the Browns' coffin when Moon hit Drew Hill for a touchdown that gave Houston its first lead and sent the largest crowd in Astrodome history into hysterics. The Oilers were now just over four minutes away from their first-ever division title. Clay Matthews sat isolated on the Cleveland sideline, just beginning to comprehend the historical ramifications that were about to crash upon him.

But the Browns, who had been knocked down countless times already in 1989, weren't done just yet. After Kosar and Co. went three-and-out, the Cleveland defense rose up with a critical stop of its own, and the beleaguered Browns offense took over at its own forty-one yard line with 2:30 to play. Following a Kosar scramble for a vital first down on third-and-one, Kevin Mack stepped into the spotlight. After spending thirty days in prison that fall for drug possession, Mack's career had teetered on the brink of collapse. Now winded and out of shape, it would be up to him to rescue the Browns, whose running attack stalled all season in his absence.

He plowed through the line for twelve yards for a first down at the Houston twenty-four, then two plays later exploded for eleven more on third-and-one, knocking Houston tacklers over as if they were bowling pins as the clock ticked down under a minute. Then Mack took another handoff from the four yard line and plowed over three tacklers and into the end zone with thirty-nine seconds remaining for the game-winning touchdown—Mack's only score of the season. Disaster had been averted. For the fourth time in five years, the Browns were AFC Central Division champions.

In the Christmas-party atmosphere of the locker room, Mack wept openly as he clung on to the football he'd scored with. In the past two months, he'd saved his life. And on an unforgettable Saturday night in the Astrodome, he also preserved Clay Matthews's legacy and saved the season for the Cleveland Browns.

	1	2	3	4	
Browns	10	7	0	7	=24
Oilers	0	3	7	10	=20

First Quarter
   CLE-Bahr 32-yd. FG
   CLE-Metcalf 68-yd. pass from Kosar (Bahr kick)
Second Quarter
   CLE-Slaughter 40-yd. pass from Kosar (Bahr kick)
   HOU-Zendejas 30-yd. FG
Third Quarter
   HOU-Hill 9-yd. pass from Moon (Zendejas kick)
Fourth Quarter
   HOU-Zendejas 37-yd. FG
   HOU-Hill 27-yd. pass from Moon (Zendejas kick)
   CLE-Mack 4-yd. run (Bahr kick)

RUSHING
CLE-Mack 12–62, Redden 6–23, Metcalf 4–14, Kosar 3–7, Manoa 1–(-1)
HOU-Pinkett 8–63, Moon 4–20, Highsmith 4–14, Rozier 3–5

PASSING
CLE-Kosar 18–36–0–228
HOU-Moon 32–51–1–414

RECEIVING
CLE-Metcalf 2–74, Slaughter 3–66, Langhorne 5–38, Brennan 4–34, McNeil
   1–6, Redden 1–6, Mack 1–3, Newsome 1–1
HOU-Hill 10–141, Duncan 7–85, Givins 5–75, Highsmith 3–40, Verhulst
   2–37, Pinkett 5–36

The King of Football

It would be a litmus test for the Browns to see if they were good enough to contend with the Giants for the Eastern Conference crown in 1959. The Cleveland defense, tops in the NFL, would face the league's best offense and its finest player on a trip to Baltimore. And as it happened, Colts quarterback Johnny Unitas would have the best statistical game of his already storied career. No one would notice, though.

The powerful Colts had won the NFL championship the year before and were on their way to a second straight title under the direction of former Browns assistant Weeb Ewbank, who had patterned the Baltimore franchise after Cleveland when he arrived in 1954. Six future Hall of Fame players would take the field for the Colts on that overcast, drizzly November afternoon at Memorial Stadium, and few expected the champs to have much trouble with 3–2 Cleveland.

After the teams traded field goals in the first quarter, the fireworks began in the second. Third-year running back Jim Brown took a pitchout on third-and-ten from his own thirty and carved through the Baltimore defense for a 70-yard touchdown. It was the opening act of what would be an unforgettable performance.

Four more touchdowns would follow for Brown, who would rack up 178 yards on thirty-two carries for the afternoon. "I do my best all the time," he said afterward, "but I just may have been hitting with a little something extra out there today." Brown would praise the performance of his blockers up front, led by Jim Ray Smith, who did a masterful job on Colts star lineman Gene "Big Daddy" Lipscomb.

All the while, Unitas and the Colt offense were having an incredible day themselves. But they simply couldn't keep up. When Baltimore tied the contest with a short Unitas–to–Lenny Moore touchdown pass, Brown broke free for a 17-yard score to make it 17–10. When the Colts threatened to score again just before the half, Bernie Parrish picked off Unitas at the Cleveland four yard line. Then early in the second half, Browns defensive back Junior Wren intercepted Unitas to set up Brown's third score. Wren came up with an even bigger theft later in the Cleveland end zone, preserving the Browns' lead.

Baltimore cut the lead to seven once again with a Raymond Berry touchdown reception with nine minutes to play. The hometown crowd began to anticipate a comeback victory. Yet appropriately, Brown clinched the contest with a one-yard touchdown plunge, capping a clutch 74-yard drive to make it 38–24 with 1:32 remaining. Though he'd broken their hearts, Brown received a standing ovation from the Baltimore fans.

Unitas added another meaningless score in the final minute, capping a remarkable performance of his own. He'd completed twenty-three passes for a team-record 397 yards and four touchdowns, but he had been overshadowed. The Browns had defeated the defending champions on their home field behind one of the greatest individual performances in the history of football. "I guess this is my most satisfying day," said Brown, who had now tallied 737 yards for the season in just six games. "There's nothing like beating the champs."

And it's not as if the champs were having an off-day. Berry snagged eleven passes for 156 yards, while Moore caught five more for 115. The teams combined for sixty-nine points and better than 800 yards of total offense. The Browns might have done even better had they not been hampered by 113 yards in penalties.

When Brown stopped by the Baltimore locker room after the game to say hello to friends Lenny Moore and Big Daddy Lipscomb, Weeb Ewbank interrupted an interview to come over to shake Brown's hand. "We knew you were quite a runner," Ewbank said, "but you're even better than we thought."

It was a realization that was about to dawn on the entire world of professional football.

	1	2	3	4	
Browns	3	14	14	7	=38
Colts	3	7	7	14	=31

First Quarter
BAL-Myhra 23-yd. FG
CLE-Groza 16-yd. FG
Second Quarter
CLE-Brown 70-yd. run (Groza kick)

BAL-Moore 5-yd. pass from Unitas (Myhra kick)
CLE-Brown 17-yd. run (Groza kick)
Third Quarter
CLE-Brown 3-yd. run (Groza kick)
BAL-Richardson 7-yd. pass from Unitas (Myhra kick)
CLE-Brown 1-yd. run (Groza kick)
Fourth Quarter
BAL-Berry 11-yd. pass from Unitas (Myhra kick)
CLE-Brown 1-yd. run (Groza kick)
BAL-Mutscheller 5-yd. pass from Unitas (Myhra kick)

RUSHING
CLE-Brown 32–178, Mitchell 8–23, Plum 2–(-4)
BAL-Ameche 9–18, Unitas 2–11, Moore 5–9, Sommer 2–6, Pricer 1–1

PASSING
CLE-Plum 14–23–2–200
BAL-Unitas 23–41–3–397

RECEIVING
CLE-Mitchell 5–66, Carpenter 3–56, Howton 3–48, Renfro 2–30, Brown
1–0
BAL-Berry 11–156, Moore 5–115, Mutscheller 4–84, Sommer 1–25, Richardson 2–17

#18

Death of The Jinx

From 1970 through the middle of the following decade, Browns fans went through life knowing there were only three things you could count on: death, taxes, and a loss in Three Rivers Stadium.

After utterly dominating the Pittsburgh Steelers no matter where they played for the first twenty years of the rivalry, a new, shadowy era began when Three Rivers opened. Suddenly, the Browns simply couldn't win in Pittsburgh. In losing the first sixteen games they played at Three Rivers, the Browns lost in every imaginable way: they were blown out (five times), shut out (once), beaten in the final two minutes (four times), and defeated in overtime (twice). By the beginning of the 1980s, the losing streak was known simply as "The Jinx."

No one could explain it. True, the Steelers were the best team in football for much of the 1970s and generally didn't lose at home to anyone. But in six of those sixteen matchups, the Browns either had a better record going in or would finish the season with a better record than the Steelers.

The Browns became as flabbergasted as their fans, brainstorming bizarre ideas to try to break The Jinx. They'd try different modes of transportation; they'd stay in different hotels. Sheer genius struck in 1985 when Browns public relations staffers brought chunks of dirt from Cleveland Stadium and sprinkled them all over the Three Rivers Astroturf. The Browns lost on a field goal with nine seconds left.

Most figured if the Browns couldn't win in Pittsburgh on this sun-soaked October Sunday in 1986, they never would. The 1–3 Steelers had plunged from their once-lofty status and now were one of the worst teams in football, having been outscored by nearly sixty points in their first four games. True to form, Pittsburgh committed a handful of mistakes in the early going of their Week

Five encounter, and the Browns surged to a 10–0 lead. Then The Jinx began to kick in. The Browns' sharp start deteriorated, and after they coughed up the ball twice in three plays, the Steelers took a 14–10 lead with just under two minutes left in the half. It looked like Part Seventeen of The Jinx was unfolding.

Then the smallest man on the field altered the course of Browns history. Tiny five-foot-nine-inch Gerald McNeil took the ensuing kickoff at his goal line and sprinted the length of the field for a 100-yard touchdown that gave the Browns back the lead and, more importantly, halted Pittsburgh's momentum. And as it happened, McNeil's touchdown—the first Cleveland kick return for a score in twelve years—would prove to be the difference.

The teams traded punches in what became a physical second-half brawl. McNeil went from hero to goat when he fumbled a punt after the Steelers' first possession, and Pittsburgh cashed in to take back the lead, 21–17. The teams traded field goals, and Pittsburgh led 24–20 early in the fourth when the Browns' special teams caught two huge breaks—the kind that always seemed to go against them at Three Rivers. First, the Steelers returned McNeil's favor by fumbling a punt that the Browns recovered at the Steeler thirty-five yard line. Then, three plays later, a missed 43-yard field goal by Matt Bahr was wiped out on a running-into-the-kicker penalty that gave Cleveland a first down. Three plays after that, Earnest Byner exploded up the middle for a four-yard touchdown to give the Browns the lead with 8:35 to play.

They were poised to tack on some insurance points with just under five minutes left, but Bahr somehow missed a 24-yard field goal after making forty straight from inside thirty yards. Browns fans rolled their eyes and covered their faces. They'd seen this before, and they hunkered down for the inevitable, painful conclusion.

Pittsburgh followed the script, driving to the Browns thirty-five with 1:38 to play, already within range for Gary Anderson to attempt the game-tying field goal. "After the missed field goal and when they started getting some first downs," Browns tackle Cody Risien said afterward, "you didn't mean to, but you were just kind of looking around like, 'God, this is the way it's happened in the past.' But we just kept saying, 'No, no, not this year, not this year.'"

"It was time for a change," Clay Matthews said. "We were going to do something big to stop what they have done for so many years."

Then came perhaps the most bizarre play call in Steeler history. On second down, quarterback Mark Malone awkwardly ran the option and fumbled on a hit by Sam Clancy. Pittsburgh running back Ernest Jackson scooped it up and ran two yards. Matthews then stripped him of the football. This time, safety

Chris Rockins recovered for the Browns at the twenty-nine yard line. After a replay review, the play stood, and the Browns had the football with ninety seconds left. They weren't out of the woods yet, though.

The Browns crossed up Pittsburgh with a gutsy 38-yard pass from Bernie Kosar to Reggie Langhorne on second down, which allowed them to run out the clock. The impossible had happened: the Browns had won their first-ever game at Three Rivers Stadium.

After sixteen years of agony, The Jinx was officially over.

	1	2	3	4	
Browns	10	7	3	7	=27
Steelers	0	14	7	3	=24

First Quarter
>   CLE-Slaughter 15-yd. pass from Kosar (Bahr kick)
>   CLE-Bahr 22-yd. FG

Second Quarter
>   PIT-Malone 1-yd. run (Anderson kick)
>   PIT-Erenberg 5-yd. pass from Malone (Anderson kick)
>   CLE-McNeil 100-yd. kickoff return (Bahr kick)

Third Quarter
>   PIT-Lipps 6-yd. pass from Malone (Anderson kick)
>   CLE-Bahr 39-yd. FG

Fourth Quarter
>   PIT-Anderson 45-yd. FG
>   CLE-Byner 4-yd. run (Bahr kick)

RUSHING
CLE-Byner 17–79, Dickey 5–21, Fontenot 5–11, Kosar 6–(-13)
PIT-Jackson 14–83, Erenberg 17–79, Abercrombie 4–19, Malone 3–2, Hughes 1–0, Lipps 1–(-7)

PASSING
CLE-Kosar 14–23–0–186
PIT-Malone 15–23–1–143

RECEIVING

CLE-Langhorne 4–108, Byner 5–29, Slaughter 2–20, Newsome 2–18, Brennan 1–11

PIT-Hughes 5–40, Gothard 2–31, Sweeney 2–29, Erenberg 3–23, Lipps 2–17, Jackson 1–3

#17

Another Doomsday for Dallas

For an entire year, the Dallas Cowboys had been thinking about revenge.

After a nearly perfect 1968 campaign in which Dallas had posted a 12–2 record, a third straight trip to the NFL Championship Game seemed certain. But the Browns had stunned the Cowboys in the Eastern Conference Championship, bringing their season to a sudden and unexpected end. Then in early November 1969, Dallas brought a 7–0 record into Cleveland for a much-anticipated rematch, and the Browns had pistol-whipped the Cowboys, 42–10—one of just two Dallas losses for the season.

Now, as both Dallas and Cleveland recovered from the harried holiday rush, their football teams prepared to crack helmets once again with a trip to the NFL title game on the line. The Browns, winners of the Century Division with a 10–3–1 mark, were six-point underdogs despite their regular-season thrashing of the Capital Division–champ Cowboys, who entered the game with surprising confidence. One reason was the Cowboys' dominating "Doomsday Defense," which had permitted less than sixteen points per game during the regular season and allowed a mere three rushing touchdowns in 1969. Speaking for the other half of the Dallas attack, quarterback Craig Morton was certain his team was ready and that this time around the Cowboys would be victorious. Morton had claimed the same thing prior to the '68 playoff. However, he explained, "I didn't sense it last time like I do this time."

In at least one sense, Morton was precisely right: it would indeed be a very different game from last year's postseason meeting, which seesawed back and forth until the Browns sealed victory in the fourth quarter. This time, on a wet, chilly day in the Cotton Bowl, the Browns utterly dominated the Dallas Cowboys.

The tone was set in the opening moments. After Dallas forced a Cleveland punt, the Cowboys fumbled the return, and Browns defensive end Bob Matheson recovered at the Dallas thirty-four yard line. It led to a short touchdown run by Bo Scott—making his third NFL start after leading the Canadian Football League in rushing four straight years—and a 7–0 Browns lead. Things would only get worse for the Cowboys.

By halftime, it was 17–0 after a Bill Nelsen touchdown pass to tight end Milt Morin and a short Don Cockroft field goal. The score would have been even worse for Dallas had Cockroft not missed two other kicks in the early going. "After we got that second touchdown, they must have said to themselves, 'This is one of those days,'" Nelsen would say later.

In the first two quarters, the Browns had out-gained Dallas 216 yards to thirty-nine and picked up fifteen first downs to the Cowboys' three. Nelsen was masterful, completing seventeen of twenty-two passes in the first half, inspiring one Dallas sportswriter to nickname him "The Master of the Third Down." Meanwhile, previously confident Craig Morton misfired on his first six pass attempts and couldn't get his team across midfield in the first thirty minutes. The hometown crowd soon began to boo and chanted for rookie Roger Staubach to relieve him. Meanwhile, fellow Dallas youngster Calvin Hill, the NFL's rookie of the year, was also contained, held to a harmless seventeen yards on eight carries on the afternoon.

Any hopes for a comeback withered on the Cowboys' first possession of the third quarter. After driving into Cleveland territory for the first time, Morton was picked off by linebacker Jim Houston, and minutes later, Scott scored again to make it 24–0. "The defense got us the ball, and we controlled it," said Cleveland offensive coach Nick Skorich. "It was bread-and-butter football. Just plain old vanilla did it."

After Leroy Kelly plowed into the end zone from the Dallas one yard line, it had taken the Browns just over three quarters to match the number of rushing touchdowns Dallas had allowed all season. Yet appropriately, it was the Cleveland defense—called a "rubber-band defense" by Dallas head coach Tom Landry earlier in the week—that provided the exclamation point early in the fourth. Down 31–7, the Cowboys were threatening to score when the rubber band snapped back. Morton was intercepted again, this time by rookie cornerback Walt Sumner at the Cleveland twelve yard line, and Sumner returned the pick eighty-eight yards for a touchdown—the longest return of the NFL season.

The final score was 38–14, as the Browns punched their ticket to their eleventh NFL title game in twenty years—their fourth under the ownership of

Art Modell, to whom the team presented a game ball for the first time. Chuck Heaton wrote that the victory "very well could be the finest pressure football game the Browns have ever played, even though they've had some great ones over the years."

Though the upset raised eyebrows all over the football world, the Browns were the only ones who didn't seem surprised. "We played the tight football we're capable of playing," Cleveland cornerback Erich Barnes said. "Nothing spectacular. We were organized, and we had pride and poise."

And that pride and poise had propelled the Browns to within one step of Super Bowl IV.

	1	2	3	4	
Browns	7	10	7	14	=38
Cowboys	0	0	7	7	=14

First Quarter
  CLE-Scott 2-yd. run (Cockroft kick)
Second Quarter
  CLE-Morin 6-yd. pass from Nelsen (Cockroft kick)
  CLE-Cockroft 29-yd. FG
Third Quarter
  CLE-Scott 2-yd. run (Cockroft kick)
  DAL-Morton 2-yd. run (Clark kick)
Fourth Quarter
  CLE-Kelly 1-yd. run (Cockroft kick)
  CLE-Sumner 88-yd. INT return (Cockroft kick)
  DAL-Rentzel 5-yd. pass from Staubach (Clark kick)

RUSHING
CLE-Kelly 19–66, Scott 11–33, Johnson 2–8, Morrison 2–3, Cockroft 1–0
DAL-Garrison 9–49, Staubach 3–22, Hill 8–17, Morton 4–12, Shay 1–0

PASSING
CLE-Nelsen 18–27–0–219, Rhome 2–2–0–35
DAL-Morton 8–24–2–92, Staubach 4–5–0–44

RECEIVING

CLE-Warfield 8–99, Morin 4–52, Scott 2–39, Collins 2–19, Morrison 1–18, Jones 1–17, Kelly 2–10

DAL-Hayes 4–44, Rentzel 3–41, Norman 1–26, Garrison 2–15, Hill 1–7, Reeves 1–3

#16

Repeat Rebuked

If you listened to Rams coach Joe Stydahar at all that week, you'd be convinced there was no need for the Browns to bother making the 3,000-mile flight to Los Angeles. After the Browns narrowly beat the Rams in the 1950 title game and then handled them easily in their regular-season rematch the following October despite having several players out to injury, Stydahar told anyone who would listen that they might as well just place the crown on the Browns' head for the second straight year.

"Jeez, we're scared to death of what's going to happen Sunday," he said. "They shouldn't have any trouble with us. . . . We weren't good enough in either of those games, so why should we be now? The Browns definitely have the better personnel and should beat us again."

By all appearances, the Rams had slipped a bit in 1951, falling to 8–4, but they were still strong enough to take the Western Conference title. The Browns, meanwhile, looked even stronger than the year before, roaring to an 11–1 record, and despite having to play on the road, they were still six-and-a-half-point favorites. But the Browns' path to a repeat title got a little bumpy on the flight west when the team plane just barely stayed ahead of a massive snowstorm barreling through Colorado. The good news was the players and coaches arrived in Los Angeles safely. The bad news was the plane carrying the team's equipment was forced to return to Denver. Consequently, the Browns had to cancel their first practice in L.A. and alter their entire preparation schedule.

Before nearly 60,000 spectators under a gorgeous California sky and—for the first time in NFL history—a nationwide television audience, the Browns and Rams resumed the back-and-forth title duel they'd begun the previous December. After a scoreless first quarter, the Rams drew first blood after a third-down pass-interference penalty on Tommy Thompson gave them a first down on the Cleveland twelve yard line. Moments later, Dick Hoerner plunged into the end zone from the one for the game's first touchdown. Lou Groza set an NFL playoff record with a 52-yard field goal, and then an Otto Graham–to–Dub Jones 17-yard touchdown pass gave Cleveland a 10–7 halftime lead.

Fueled by uncharacteristic generosity on the part of the Browns, the Rams surged back ahead. First, defensive end Andy Robustelli returned a Graham fumble to the Cleveland one yard line, and Dan Towler scored to make it 14–10. Momentum swung back and forth like a giant brass pendulum. A 52-yard touchdown pass from Graham to Mac Speedie was called back on a holding penalty on Groza, then the Rams' Norm Van Brocklin—who replaced ineffective quarterback Bob Waterfield—connected with wideout Tom Fears for a 48-yard pass to the Cleveland one. But the Browns defense pushed the Rams back to the eighteen and then snuffed out a fake field-goal attempt.

On the ensuing possession, Marv Johnson intercepted Graham and scampered to the Browns one yard line, where Los Angeles would again have first and goal. Once again, however, the Cleveland defense rose to the occasion, forcing Los Angeles to settle for a field goal that boosted the margin to 17–10 three minutes into the fourth quarter. The Browns responded with a clutch ten-play, 70-yard drive keyed by a 34-yard run by Graham and capped by a 5-yard touchdown run over right tackle by Ken Carpenter that tied the contest with 7:50 remaining. The energetic Los Angeles crowd and television viewers across the country prepared for another climactic championship-game finish. And they got it.

Twenty-five seconds after Carpenter's score, Fears snuck behind Cleveland cornerback Tommy James and reeled in a long, looping third-down pass from the Ram twenty-seven yard line. Fears caught what he would later call the best-thrown pass he'd ever seen at the Cleveland forty and sprinted the remaining yards into the end zone to give the Rams a 24–17 advantage as they cashed in on the Browns' only big defensive mistake of the day. Things looked even bleaker for the Browns on the next play from scrimmage when Ram linebacker Don Paul picked off Graham and returned the ball to the Cleveland fourteen yard line with under seven minutes to play. It was Graham's third interception of the afternoon, and it appeared it would cost the Browns the game.

But as they'd done all afternoon, the Browns wouldn't allow Los Angeles to put the game away. Two minutes later, Bill Willis broke through the line to block a 23-yard field-goal attempt by Waterfield, and the Browns regained possession at their own thirty-eight yard line. They picked up a first down at their own forty-nine then were faced with fourth-and-two at the Rams forty-three with three minutes showing. The call was a pitch to Dub Jones sweeping around left end, but Los Angeles defensive back Herb Rich tripped up Jones for a two-yard loss, and the Rams took over. The Browns wouldn't see the ball again until ten seconds remained, and it wasn't enough time.

For the first time in seven years, the city of Cleveland would not celebrate a professional football championship as the Browns lost the first truly heart-breaking game in team history. Suffice it to say, many more would follow.

	1	2	3	4	
Browns	0	10	0	7	=17
Rams	0	7	7	10	=24

Second Quarter
  LA-Hoerner 1-yd. run (Waterfield kick)
  CLE-Groza 52-yd. FG
  CLE-Jones 17-yd. pass from Graham (Groza kick)
Third Quarter
  LA-Towler 2-yd. run (Waterfield kick)
Fourth Quarter
  LA-Waterfield 17-yd. FG
  CLE-Carpenter 5-yd. run (Groza kick)
  LA-Fears 73-yd. pass from Van Brocklin (Waterfield kick)

RUSHING
CLE-Graham 5–43, Motley 5–23, Carpenter 4–14, Jones 9–12
LA-Towler 16–36, Younger 4–20, Smith 9–15, Waterfield 2–8, Davis 6–6,
  Hoerner 5–5, Van Brocklin 1–3

PASSING
CLE-Graham 19–40–3–280, Carpenter 0–1–0–0
LA-Van Brocklin 4–6–0–128, Waterfield 9–23–2–125

RECEIVING
CLE-Speedie 7–81, Lavelli 4–65, Jones 4–62, Carpenter 3–49, Motley 1–23
LA-Fears 4–146, Hirsch 4–66, Smith 1–18, Hoerner 1–13, Davis 3–10

the *Monday Night* cameras, across the nation. "It came as a tremendous lift just to come out onto the field," Brian Sipe said. "There is something magical about it. There is no place in the world like Cleveland and the Stadium on a night when it is full of our fans. It is a feeling that is hard to describe."

Even enigmatic broadcaster Howard Cosell was impressed in the ABC booth. "I haven't seen this kind of excitement in this ballpark since 1948 when the Indians won their first pennant in twenty-eight years," he said. "Excitement prevails in this usually troubled city. The people believe in this team."

In the first seven minutes, the team put on a show its fans would never forget.

The Browns exploded for three quick touchdowns, each more dazzling than the one before. First, after taking the opening kickoff and driving to the Dallas twenty-three yard line, Sipe looped a pass down the left sideline, which Dave Logan caught in the end zone for a 6–0 lead. Two plays after forcing a Dallas punt, Sipe picked up right where he left off, scrambling away from the Cowboy rush and launching a 48-yard scoring pass to Ozzie Newsome. The best was yet to come, though.

Just over ninety seconds later, Thom Darden made good on a promise he'd made the previous week, ending Roger Staubach's quest to break the NFL record for most consecutive passes without an interception. Darden picked off a Staubach pass at the Dallas thirty-nine and sprinted untouched into the end zone for another touchdown. It was 20–0, and the rout was on.

The final was 26–7, the Cowboys' worst loss in seven years. Darden picked off another pass, Curtis Weathers blocked a field goal, and the Browns recovered three fumbles and pinned Staubach four times—three and a half by Jerry Sherk, who also recovered one of the fumbles. "We got a lead, but we didn't sit on it," Rutigliano explained. "We kept going at them."

In so doing, the Browns reintroduced themselves to the NFL. "You don't beat a club as tempered and well-coached as Dallas so convincingly unless you've got talent, pride and desire on your side," Hal Lebovitz wrote. "The Browns had it all last night. . . . There was some doubt in this corner about whether they could play with the big boys. There is no doubt any longer."

The only thing that went wrong for the Browns came after the final gun sounded, when defensive end Lyle Alzado tripped over a security guard trying to clear a path through the mob of fans that had rushed the field. Alzado fell down the stairs of the dugout and bruised his knee.

The crowd's exuberance could be excused, though. It had, after all, been a long decade. "The town and team deserve this moment of glory," Lebovitz eloquently wrote.

But Cosell put it best: "What a night for Cleveland!"

	1	2	3	4	
Cowboys	7	0	0	0	= 7
Browns	20	0	0	6	=26

First Quarter
   CLE-Logan 23-yd. pass from Sipe (kick failed)
   CLE-Newsome 48-yd. pass from Sipe (Cockroft kick)
   CLE-Darden 39-yd. INT return (Cockroft kick)
   DAL-Hill 48-yd. pass from Staubach (Septien kick)
Fourth Quarter
   CLE-M. Pruitt 2-yd. run (kick blocked)

RUSHING

DAL-Dorsett 14–64, Laidlaw 13–49, Staubach 2–11, DuPree 1–(-1)

CLE-M. Pruitt 14–31, Hill 7–24, G. Pruitt 6–15, Miller 2–7, Moriarty 2–5,
   Sipe 1–1, Feacher 1–(-1)

PASSING

DAL-Staubach 21–39–2–303
CLE-Sipe 15–28–1–239

RECEIVING

DAL-D. Pearson 5–109, Hill 3–70, P. Pearson 3–34, DuPree 3–29, Wilson
   1–21, Saidi 1–15, Laidlaw 3–9, Dorsett 1–9, Cosbie 1–7
CLE-Rucker 5–57, Miller 3–55, Newsome 3–53, Logan 2–42, G. Pruitt 1–27,
   M. Pruitt 1–5

#14

BROWNS 26, PITTSBURGH STEELERS 24
NOVEMBER 19, 1972

Cockroft's Redemption

After four decades of ineptitude, the Pittsburgh Steelers had suddenly exploded into the upper echelon of professional football. From the depths of a 1–13 season in Chuck Noll's first campaign as head coach three years before, the Steelers were on the brink of a dynasty. "There is something about us now that makes me feel different," Pittsburgh running back John Fuqua said going into Week Ten of the 1972 season. That feeling was not only correct, it would alter the course of football history.

Under the leadership of Noll and sparked by an up-and-coming defense led by lineman Joe Greene and linebackers Andy Russell and Dwight White, Pittsburgh steamrolled to a 7–2 start in '72, one victory away from clinching its first winning record in nine years. While the defense had become dominant, carrying the team to the threshold of its eventual "Steel Curtain" moniker, it was the arrival of rookie running back Franco Harris on the other side of the ball which had raised the Steelers to a championship-caliber level. Harris, who would rush for better than a thousand yards for the year while averaging nearly six yards per carry, was already being compared to Cleveland legend Jim Brown.

Riding a five-game winning streak, the Steelers would take the "six-pack drive along the Turnpike"—as described by Hal Lebovitz—to battle the 6–3 Browns for first place in the AFC Central on a cold, rainy day along the shores of Lake Erie. The Browns, defending division champs, were also on a roll, having won four in a row themselves—the latest a last-minute, Monday-night victory in San Diego. A crowd of better than 83,000 would pack Cleveland Stadium for the biggest Browns-Steelers game in the twenty-three-year history of the rivalry.

On a muddy, torn-up field that symbolized the rugged turn the rivalry was about to take, the Browns and Steelers matched one another blow for blow.

With Mike Phipps directing an offense running on all cylinders, the Browns surged to a 20–3 second-quarter lead, only to see it evaporate. Terry Bradshaw drove his team eighty-seven yards in the final forty-nine seconds of the half and tossed a touchdown pass to cut the margin to ten. Then Fuqua capped a Pittsburgh drive to make it 23–17 late in the third.

With time running out, Franco Harris broke free for the first of what would be many long runs against the Cleveland defense in his career. After being contained all afternoon, Harris slipped through the Browns and sloshed through the mud for a 75-yard touchdown scamper to give Pittsburgh a 24–23 lead.

With hopes for the division title fading fast, the Browns responded. Sparked by a brilliant third-down bootleg run by Phipps that earned sixteen yards and a first down, Cleveland drove to the Pittsburgh nineteen yard line with just under two minutes remaining. Nick Skorich called on Don Cockroft, the most accurate kicker in football, to give the Browns back the lead with a chip-shot field goal. Inexplicably, Cockroft missed wide left from twenty-seven yards, giving the Steelers the football back with a chance to run out the clock. High above the field in the press box, Lebovitz scribbled, "The whole season went down the drain with that miss" in his notebook. Cockroft returned to the sideline despondent, where he began praying for a second chance.

The Browns defense rose up, however, forcing Pittsburgh into a third-and-short situation with a minute left. Nick Roman and Jerry Sherk pummeled Bradshaw on a rollout for a loss, and the Steelers were forced to punt. After Leroy Kelly returned the kick to the Cleveland forty-two yard line with fifty-two seconds remaining, Phipps took over. Sliding through the mud, he hit wideout Fair Hooker over the middle for seventeen yards, and then connected with Frank Pitts on a post pattern for eighteen more. After the Steelers were penalized for being offside, the Browns were at the Pittsburgh eighteen with thirteen seconds to play. Cockroft was sent out again to try to win the game from almost the precise spot where he'd apparently lost it just over a minute before.

This time, Cockroft came through, calmly pushing the football through the uprights to secure one of the Browns' most dramatic victories. Never before had Cleveland scored game-winning points with so little time left on the clock, and the kicker was mobbed by his teammates as he left the field.

"I knew I'd get a second chance," a jubilant Cockroft said. "It was the greatest thrill of my football career."

	1	2	3	4	
Steelers	3	7	7	7	=24
Browns	10	10	3	3	=26

First Quarter
    PIT-Gerela 39-yd. FG
    CLE-Cockroft 26-yd. FG
    CLE-Phipps 1-yd. run (Cockroft kick)
Second Quarter
    CLE-Cockroft 38-yd. FG
    CLE-Pitts 17-yd. pass from Phipps (Cockroft kick)
    PIT-Mullins 3-yd. pass from Bradshaw (Gerela kick)
Third Quarter
    CLE-Cockroft 12-yd. FG
    PIT-Fuqua 1-yd. run (Gerela kick)
Fourth Quarter
    PIT-Harris 75-yd. run (Gerela kick)
    CLE-Cockroft 26-yd. FG

RUSHING
PIT-Harris 12–136, Fuqua 13–46, Bradshaw 3–17, Lewis 1–12
CLE-Kelly 21–107, Scott 14–84, Phipps 3–26

PASSING
PIT-Bradshaw 10–21–1–136
CLE-Phipps 14–25–2–194

RECEIVING
PIT-Shanklin 5–108, Lewis 3–24, Mullins 1–3, Harris 1–1
CLE-Morin 4–77, Pitts 3–43, Hooker 2–25, Glass 2–24, Scott 2–15, Kelly
    1–10

#13

DETROIT LIONS 17, BROWNS 16
DECEMBER 27, 1953

Some Kind of Hex

"The Browns probably haven't been captivated with so fierce a thirst for victory since they played the Los Angeles Rams in 1950."

Harold Sauerbrei's words summed up the atmosphere surrounding the Cleveland Browns during Christmas week, 1953. While it would be an overstatement to say they were desperate for a victory in that Sunday's NFL Championship at Detroit's Briggs Stadium, clearly the Browns had something to prove.

After storming into the NFL in 1950 and winning a thrilling championship contest over the Rams, the Browns fought back to the title game the next two years but lost both times after disappointing performances. A loss at home to Detroit in '52 was the hardest to take, as the Browns squandered numerous scoring opportunities and essentially handed the game to the Lions. Now, a year later, they'd have a shot at redemption.

Most fans and sportswriters saw the 1953 rematch as a toss-up. Each team had a superstar quarterback (Otto Graham and Bobby Layne) leading a potent offense, and both units had accumulated better than 4,000 yards during the season. Both the 10–2 Lions and 11–1 Browns boasted four receivers who had caught twenty or more passes, and the two defenses had been the best in football. Accordingly, the consensus was that the outcome would be determined not by which team had the better talent, but by which caught the bigger breaks. In the previous five meetings between the teams, including an exhibition contest, Detroit had caught seemingly every break, winning four and tying another, though there was only a twenty-seven-point difference in the quintet of games.

With a crowd of 54,577 on hand (including better than 3,000 fans from Cleveland who had taken special trains the night before) on a sunny but cold afternoon, the Lions caught the first break. On the second play of the game, Graham was hit by lineman LaVern Torgeson and fumbled. Detroit's Les Bingaman recovered on the Cleveland thirteen yard line. It set the tone for what would become the worst game of Graham's storied career. Six plays later, it was 7–0, Lions.

Though the Browns kept the game close, Graham just couldn't get going. He would complete only two of fifteen passes on the day for a mere four yards. "I was lousy, and I admit it," he would say later. "I wish I could play that one all over." At one point, Graham instructed Paul Brown to take him out of the game and replace him with backup George Ratterman. Though Ratterman completed an 18-yard pass, the going wasn't any easier, and Brown soon reverted back to Graham.

Still, the Browns stayed in the game. Len Ford recovered a fumble at the Detroit six late in the first quarter that led to a field goal—though it could have been more had Dante Lavelli not slipped and dropped a third-down pass in the end zone. Detroit caught another break in the last two minutes of the half when a Graham pass went through Ken Carpenter's hands and was intercepted by Jim David to set up a short Doak Walker field goal to make it 10–3 at intermission. Despite only managing seventy-one yards of offense in the first half, the Browns only trailed by a touchdown. And when Ken Gorgal intercepted Layne on the third play of the third quarter, the momentum began to swing.

The Browns drove fifty-one yards in eight plays, and Chick Jagade tied the contest with a 9-yard scoring run. With the Cleveland defense continuing to thwart Layne and the Lions, the Browns managed to take the lead with a pair of Lou Groza field goals in the fourth. The second put Cleveland ahead 16–10 with 4:10 to play, and the Browns, incredibly, were on the brink of their second NFL championship.

But the Lions weren't done. Layne drove his offense eighty yards in eight plays, twice hitting little-used substitute Jim Doran for big gains. Then, after Doran suggested going long, he snuck behind the Browns' Warren Lahr and reeled in a 33-yard touchdown pass to tie the contest with 2:08 showing. Walker, who had missed two field goals earlier, came through with the crucial extra point, and the Lions led by one.

While there was enough time left for the Browns to respond, Graham's horrific day continued. On the first play of the ensuing possession, he was picked off by rookie defensive back Carl Karilivacz, and the Lions killed the clock, becoming just the third team in NFL history to win back-to-back titles. "I know we're better than they are," Graham said. "They played a lousy game, but we stunk out the joint."

Uncharacteristically, the press was not allowed in the Cleveland locker room immediately after the game was over, as Paul Brown called for a fifteen-minute "cooling-off period." When reporters were permitted inside, they found a despondent Brown. "Well, it's part of living," he repeated over and over as if trying to convince himself. "We have lost before, and we'll lose again."

Yet the Browns' reputation now seemed sullied. Despite losing just six times in the previous three regular seasons, they'd now dropped three straight title games. "For the third successive year," Gordon Cobbledick wrote, "they, like their cousins, the Indians, were proved to be merely second-best."

This loss also proved that for whatever reason, the Lions clearly had the Browns' number, once again confirming "the indisputable truth that Detroit holds some kind of hex over the Browns," Sauerbrei wrote.

All the Browns could do was look toward 1954, when they would try to restore their pride and shake the rap of a team that couldn't win the big game. "There used to be a time when we were like the New York Yankees," Brown said. "Anything we did turned out right for us. But I guess that's life. . . . They gave one tremendous effort. We simply made the big mistakes; that's all.

"Nobody'll ever lose a tougher one."

Perhaps not. But generations of Browns teams to come would try to prove him wrong.

	1	2	3	4	
Browns	0	3	7	6	=16
Lions	7	3	0	7	=17

First Quarter
DET-Walker 1-yd. run (Walker kick)
Second Quarter
CLE-Groza 14-yd. FG
DET-Walker 23-yd. FG
Third Quarter
CLE-Jagade 9-yd. run (Groza kick)
Fourth Quarter
CLE-Groza 15-yd. FG
CLE-Groza 43-yd. FG
DET-Doran 33-yd. pass from Layne (Walker kick)

RUSHING
CLE-Jagade 15–102, Jones 3–28, Reynolds 6–17, Carpenter 3–15, Renfro 4–11, Graham 5–9
DET-Hoernschemeyer 17–51, Layne 9–44, Gedman 8–29, Walker 3–5

Passing
CLE-Graham 2–15–2–20, Ratterman 1–1–0–18
DET-Layne 12–25–2–179

Receiving
CLE-Jagade 1–18, Lavelli 1–13, Reynolds 1–7
DET-Doran 4–95, Box 4–54, Dibble 1–22, Walker 1–10, Hoernschemeyer
  2–2

#12

OAKLAND RAIDERS 14, BROWNS 12
JANUARY 4, 1981

Frozen Moment

It was as if Mother Nature appreciated the historical significance of what was about to happen and wanted to leave her own mark.

As a vicious cold front began to march toward Northeast Ohio in the first week of 1981, the city of Cleveland was intoxicated with the Kardiac Kids. In the two weeks since the Browns had clinched their first division title in nine years, local merchants couldn't keep Browns merchandise on their shelves. "The Twelve Days of a Cleveland Browns Christmas" played endlessly on the radio, and the players were pursued like rock stars. Now, as the city geared up for the Browns' divisional playoff against the Oakland Raiders, that cold front slammed down upon it like a giant freezer door. Clevelanders awoke that Sunday morning to thermometers hovering near zero, with a slicing wind off the lake dropping the chill factor to nearly forty below.

Still, the majority of the 77,000 fans who trudged into Cleveland Stadium didn't mind the cold. They were sure their Kardiac Kids would keep them warm. But having to contend with the frozen, marble-like field and gusting winds, neither team could assert itself early on, and the game took on a surreal tone.

After the teams exchanged seven punts and a pair of interceptions in the first quarter, the Browns caught the first break of the day when cornerback Ron Bolton picked off Oakland quarterback Jim Plunkett and carefully maneuvered forty-two yards for the game's first touchdown six minutes before the half. Appropriately, Don Cockroft missed the ensuing extra point, so the Browns' lead stayed at six. It was an ominous portent.

The Browns had multiple opportunities to build up their advantage in the first half, but they all went awry. Reggie Rucker dropped a certain touchdown pass to close the first quarter, then couldn't stop his momentum and slid down the steps leading to one of the baseball dugouts. The Browns drove to the Oakland twenty-nine yard line to start the second quarter, but Cockroft was short on a 48-yard field-goal attempt. Cleveland's Marshall Harris recovered a Plunkett fumble at the Oakland twenty-three, but Cockroft missed a 30-yard kick. After dodging bullets throughout the first half, the Raiders surged ahead 7–6 at the intermission.

Brian Sipe and the Cleveland offense gradually adjusted to the conditions in the second half and embarked on three lengthy drives that resulted in a pair of Cockroft field goals and a 12–7 lead. The advantage could have been more, but a bad snap foiled a 36-yard attempt midway through the third quarter. Oakland surged back ahead with a short Mark van Eeghan touchdown run midway through the fourth. Things looked even grimmer for the home team a few minutes later when Brian Sipe fumbled and the Raiders recovered at the Cleveland twenty-four yard line with 4:23 remaining.

The embattled Cleveland defense rose to the occasion, however, stuffing van Eeghan on a gutsy fourth-and-inches attempt at the fifteen with 2:22 left. Sipe and Co. returned to the field, and every Browns fan knew exactly what was going to happen next. *"They are ready for another Cleveland Browns finish,"* Don Criqui told his NBC audience. *"Fasten all seat belts."*

"This is it," Sipe told his teammates in the huddle. "Here's where we win the game." Just as they'd done on almost a weekly basis over the previous two seasons, the Browns were headed for a dramatic last-minute climax. Sipe connected with Ozzie Newsome for twenty-nine yards then hit Greg Pruitt for twenty-three more to the Raider twenty-eight yard line. On the next play, the Browns surprised Oakland with a draw to fullback Mike Pruitt that gathered fourteen yards and gave them a first down at the fourteen yard line with under a minute to play.

After Pruitt plowed forward for another yard, the Browns called time-out with forty-nine seconds left. The Browns had a decision to make: play it safe and try to win the game with a field goal or go for the touchdown. On a normal day, conventional football wisdom demanded the former. But Cockroft had been affected by the lousy conditions more than any other player, missing four of the six kicks he attempted. Sam Rutigliano opted to roll the dice just as he'd done successfully several times each of the past two seasons.

The play call was "Red Right 88." Sipe dropped back, looking for Dave Logan crossing over the middle. When he found Logan covered, he instead fired a pass to his left for Ozzie Newsome in the end zone. But, in the split second that decision was made, Oakland's Dwayne O'Steen abandoned coverage on Logan to help fellow cornerback Mike Davis with Newsome. It left Logan wide open and Newsome double-teamed. "He thought he saw Ozzie open," Rutigliano would say later. "The next time we looked at the film, Dave Logan is wide open in the end zone. The rest is history."

The ball wobbled through the arctic air and settled into the arms of Davis, who tumbled to the ground with the biggest interception in Raider history.

The rabid cheers of the sellout crowd evaporated, their dreams snuffed out like a candle. "It was very surreal," Browns safety Thom Darden said. "It was almost as if it was a dream, and it wasn't really happening. Like a nightmare."

The clock had struck midnight on the magical 1980 season, and the reign of the Kardiac Kids had come to a sudden, heart-wrenching conclusion.

Rutigliano never second-guessed himself, though. "I never worried about that," he said. "Matter of fact, I have a lot of fun with it. Which is I think the way it's supposed to be."

Looking back through the filter of history, what ending would have better fit the Kardiac Kids?

	1	2	3	4	
Raiders	0	7	0	7	=14
Browns	0	6	6	0	=12

Second Quarter
   CLE-Bolton 42-yd. INT return (kick failed)
   OAK-van Eeghan 2-yd. run (Bahr kick)
Third Quarter
   CLE-Cockroft 30-yd. FG
   CLE-Cockroft 36-yd. FG
Fourth Quarter
   OAK-van Eeghan 1-yd. run (Bahr kick)

RUSHING

OAK-van Eeghan 20–45, King 12–23, Plunkett 4–8, Whittington 1–1, Jensen 1–(-1)

CLE-M. Pruitt 13–48, Hill 2–23, Sipe 6–13, G. Pruitt 4–11, Miller 1–1, Mc-Donald 1–(-11)

PASSING

OAK-Plunkett 14–30–2–149
CLE-Sipe 13–40–3–183

RECEIVING

OAK-Chester 3–64, van Eeghan 3–23, Branch 2–23, Chandler 1–15, King 4–14, Whittington 1–10

CLE-G. Pruitt 3–54, Newsome 4–51, Rucker 2–38, Logan 2–36, Hill 2–4

#11

BROWNS 8, NEW YORK GIANTS 3
DECEMBER 17, 1950

Birth of a Rivalry

The Browns' inaugural season in the NFL had been nearly perfect. They'd won ten games, including a pair over the two-time defending champion Philadelphia Eagles. In their victories, they'd outscored their opponents by an average of more than seventeen points per game and outgained them by more than a thousand yards. In just three months, they'd redefined the world of professional football and had begun one of the most successful eras in the history of sports.

There had been just one stain on this near-flawless 1950 campaign: a blue-and-white smear known as the New York Giants.

The Giants had been the only team to defeat the Browns that fall, and they'd done it twice: a 6–0 defensive slugfest at Cleveland Stadium and a narrow 17–13 decision at the Polo Grounds three weeks later. Like the Browns, New York finished with a 10–2 record, which left them knotted atop the American Conference. It set up just the fourth-ever playoff in league history—with the winner advancing to the NFL Championship Game. Such a dramatic encounter was nothing new for the Giants and veteran coach Steve Owens, who was gunning for his ninth title-game appearance in twenty years.

Both teams knew precisely what to expect. "This should be the same savage kind of football game we played them the last two times," Browns coach Paul Brown predicted. While the Giant offense had been hot down the stretch, the Browns' biggest challenge would be putting points on the board after being dominated by the New York defense in their two earlier meetings. Ironically, though the Giants had experience on their side and the two regular-season victories under their belt, the Browns were considered slight favorites. The primary reason, most believed, was simple motivation; the Browns had become obsessed with defeating the Giants to prove they were indeed the finest team in football. Though they'd dominated the All-American Football Conference, "always there was the ambition to meet the best from the National League to make the claim stand up," Harold Sauerbrei wrote.

Another justification for the Browns' confidence, conjectured Sauerbrei, was one man. "You also have to like the Browns' chances to gain revenge . . . if for no other reason than they have Lou Groza," Sauerbrei wrote. "The weather is sure to be a big factor and with a player of Groza's ability it could give the Browns a decided advantage."

Though the Giants defeated the Browns twice in the regular season, Cleveland would host the playoff by winning a fateful coin flip. And on the edge of Lake Erie in late December, the weather would be a factor, as the temperature hovered in the teens and the wind howled in off the lake on the fourteenth consecutive day of snowfall in the Cleveland area. A modest crowd of 33,054 filed into Cleveland Stadium to witness one of the most titanic defensive struggles in NFL history. With the field frozen as solid as concrete, players from both sides wore rubber-soled shoes to keep from slipping. It worked like a charm for the Browns in the opening minutes, as they took the opening kickoff and marched inside the Giant five yard line, coming away with a short Groza field goal and a 3–0 lead.

There the score would remain through the frosty second and third quarters, as the Browns defense dominated New York, preventing the Giants from crossing midfield until the second half. Then, midway through the fourth quarter, New York caught a break and was suddenly poised to clinch victory. With ten minutes remaining, Giants tailback Gene Roberts scampered around right end at the Browns thirty-six yard line and found daylight. He cut inside the Cleveland ten and appeared certain to score. Then Browns defensive end Bill Willis made a flying desperation tackle from behind to stop Roberts at the four yard line. "I thought he was away for a touchdown," Willis admitted later. "All I could think of was that number on Roberts' back represented the championship running away from me." For as brilliant as Willis's play had been, it seemed his effort would be for naught, since New York had a first down twelve feet from the end zone. A touchdown would all but secure another trip to the NFL Championship for the Giants.

The fans sunk into their seats, feeling colder than they had all day. But in the next few moments, they stood up again and, for the first time in Browns history, began a synchronized chant. "Hold that line!" they cried over and over again as the Giants marched up to the line of scrimmage. The Browns, not wanting to disappoint their frozen faithful, dutifully complied.

Willis came up big again, twice stopping running plays. Then, in the next minute, both teams appeared to clinch victory. First, New York quarterback Chuck Conerly hit Bob McChesney with a pass in the end zone, but the play was called back on a Giant penalty. Then Browns defensive back Tommy James intercepted Conerly, only to have that play wiped out on a Cleveland infraction. After Willis smothered Joe Scott for a five-yard loss, and linebacker Jim Martin knocked down Conerly's third-down pass, the Giants were forced to settle for a game-tying 20-yard field goal by Randall Clay. Altogether, New York had seven snaps from inside the Cleveland thirteen yard line to try to win the game, and the Browns had kept them from scoring a touchdown.

With just 6:10 remaining, most of the frozen spectators prepared themselves for the NFL's first-ever overtime game. Instead, they were about to witness what would forever be remembered as one of the most dramatic finishes in Browns history. Dominic Moselle returned the ensuing kickoff twenty-nine yards to the Cleveland thirty-five, then Otto Graham took control of the contest. He scampered nine yards on first down, then a play later, covered fifteen more to the New York forty yard line. A play after that, Graham faked a handoff then spun through the middle of the line for twelve yards. With the clock ticking down under two minutes, halfback Rex Bumgardner clawed to the Giant twenty-two, and with the season hanging in the balance, Paul Brown called on Lou Groza to boot the Browns into their first NFL title game.

Groza, who had replaced the cleats on his kicking shoe with rubber soles in anticipation of just such a kick, didn't disappoint. Though Brown would later confess it was "one of the tensest moments of my life," Groza coolly booted a 29-yard field goal with fifty-eight seconds remaining to give the Browns a 6–3 lead. As Sauerbrei had predicted the day before, Groza was the difference.

Appropriately, the Browns defense put the exclamation point on the victory. Martin chased a desperate Conerly into the end zone and pinned him there for a safety with eight seconds left (though Willis would be credited in the box score). It made the final 8–3, and it didn't go unnoticed in Cleveland that the score was identical to the Indians' American League playoff with the Boston Red Sox that sent the Tribe to the World Series two years earlier.

For as much attention as the Browns' new-age offense had received throughout the season, it was the defense that had propelled the newcomers to the title game. And the ringleader was Willis, who was just as dominant as he'd been in his days playing for Brown at Ohio State. "Willis is the greatest lineman in American football," Brown proclaimed after the game. "He gave a superb performance."

As a result, the Browns could look forward to a Christmas Eve showdown with the equally potent Los Angeles Rams for the 1950 championship. Not only had the Browns earned their revenge over the Giants, they'd also begun one of the greatest rivalries in the history of professional football.

	1	2	3	4	
Giants	0	0	0	3	=3
Browns	3	0	0	5	=8

First Quarter
    CLE-Groza 11-yd. FG
Fourth Quarter
    NY-Clay 20-yd. FG
    CLE-Groza 29-yd. FG
    CLE-Safety: Willis tackled Conerly in end zone

RUSHING
CLE-Graham 8–70, Bumgardner 13–39, Jones 12–32, Motley 7–12

PASSING
NY-Conerly 3–15–2–48
CLE-Graham 3–8–1–43

RECEIVING
NY-McChesney 1–19, Roberts 1–17, Sulaitis 1–12
CLE-Lavelli 2–35, Bumgardner 1–8

#10

BROWNS 31, DALLAS COWBOYS 20
DECEMBER 21, 1968

Proud to Be a Brown

As the 1968 regular season came to a close, most football fans were in concurrence with one standard observation: the Dallas Cowboys were about to become the NFL's next dynasty.

The Cowboys had reached the NFL Championship each of the previous two seasons, losing heartbreaking last-minute decisions to Green Bay each time. But the '68 Cowboys were even better, boasting the league's top offense and second-best defense, which they parlayed to a 12–2 record and a Capital Division title. Coach Tom Landry called it his best team ever. As the playoffs began, much of the sporting world was already looking forward to an epic NFL title-game clash between Dallas and 13–1 Baltimore.

No one expected the Browns to give the mighty Cowboys much of a game in the divisional playoff—and with good reason: Dallas had steamrolled to a 28–7 victory over Cleveland in Week Two and spanked the Browns by thirty-eight points in the playoffs a year earlier. The Cowboys had defeated the Browns four straight times and coasted into the playoffs riding a five-game winning streak. Cleveland, meanwhile, had rallied from a sluggish start to go 10–4 and win the Century Division for the second straight year. After newly acquired backup Bill Nelsen had replaced ineffective Frank Ryan at quarterback, the Browns had ripped off eight straight victories—their longest winning streak in fourteen years. While it was certainly a season to be proud of, most of the 81,000 fans that filed into Cleveland Stadium on the shortest day of the year figured they were coming to see the Cowboys close the books on the '68 Browns.

But, in the moments before kickoff, as the team gathered in the haunting silence of the locker room, an unlikely orator stepped to the proverbial podium. Little-used wide receiver Tommy McDonald, who had caught just seven

161

passes all season after coming out of retirement to help patch the Browns' injury-riddled receiving corps, began to speak. "I didn't earn my way here," he started softly. "I'm here because Gary Collins got hurt. But I'm proud to be wearing this uniform. I'm proud to be a Brown."

By the time he was done, the entire team was flooded with emotion and screaming. "It was like Knute Rockne," Collins said. "It was one of the most inspirational speeches I've ever heard." Added Dick Schafrath: "We wanted to win this one as bad as any game in our lives."

The Cleveland defense, which was supposed to be simply overwhelmed by the Cowboy attack, set the tone early when a Mike Howell interception of Don Meredith led to a Don Cockroft field goal. Dallas stole the momentum back when linebacker Chuck Howley returned a Nelsen fumble forty-four yards for the go-ahead touchdown. The Stadium crowd was silenced, as it appeared the Cowboys' march to inevitable victory had begun.

Dallas stretched its lead to 10–3 in the second quarter then pinned the Browns at their own fifteen yard line in the waning moments of the half. But Nelsen drove Cleveland to the Dallas forty-five with a minute showing then hit Leroy Kelly for a lightning-like 45-yard touchdown pass to tie the contest. Things would only get better for the home team after intermission.

Starting with Kelly's score, the Browns racked up three touchdowns in just over three minutes of play. On the first play of the second half, linebacker Dale Lindsey batted a Meredith pass up into the air, juggled it, then hung on and returned it twenty-seven yards to give the Browns the lead. Three plays later, Meredith was picked off again—this time by Ben Davis. A snap after that, Kelly took a handoff on a sweep and curled around end and into the clear for a 35-yard touchdown to make it 24–10. The crowd went bonkers.

Trailing by eleven in the fourth, the Cowboys clawed to the Cleveland thirty yard line and were poised to pull within a touchdown. But Erich Barnes intercepted Craig Morton—who'd relieved Meredith midway through the third quarter. Nelsen then connected with Paul Warfield for a 39-yard pass to set up a back-breaking touchdown run by Ernie Green with just over five minutes remaining.

Even without its four interceptions, the Cleveland defense was suffocating. The Browns utterly dominated the best offense in the game, holding Dallas to just eighty-six rushing yards and twelve completions in thirty-two pass attempts while containing star wideouts Bob Hayes and Lance Rentzel. Time and time again, the crowd gave the defense standing ovations as it came off the field.

With just over a minute to play and the Browns up 31–20, many fans began climbing out of the stands and, when the clock hit zero, rushed the field to celebrate one of the biggest upsets in team history. "They had beaten us four times in a row, and we were tired of it," linebacker Jim Houston said. "I've said before this is the greatest Browns team I've ever played on. I guess I'd have to say this is the greatest game. Everyone took it on themselves to win it."

	1	2	3	4	
Cowboys	7	3	3	7	=20
Browns	3	7	14	7	=31

First Quarter
    CLE-Cockroft 38-yd. FG
    DAL-Howley 44-yd. fumble return (Clark kick)
Second Quarter
    DAL-Clark 16-yd. FG
    CLE-Kelly 45-yd. pass from Nelsen (Cockroft kick)
Third Quarter
    CLE-Lindsey 27-yd. INT return (Cockroft kick)
    CLE-Kelly 35-yd. run (Cockroft kick)
    DAL-Clark 47-yd. FG
Fourth Quarter
    CLE-Green 2-yd. run (Cockroft kick)
    DAL-Garrison 2-yd. pass from Morton (Clark kick)

RUSHING
DAL-Perkins 14–51, Morton 2–14, Baynham 10–7, Garrison 1–6, Meredith
    1–5, Shy 2–3
CLE-Kelly 20–87, Harraway 5–12, Green 3–5, Nelsen 2–(-2)

PASSING
DAL-Morton 9–23–1–163, Meredith 3–9–3–42
CLE-Nelsen 13–25–1–203

RECEIVING
DAL-Hayes 5–83, Rentzel 3–75, Baynham 1–34, Garrison 2–8, Norman 1–5
CLE-Warfield 4–86, Morin 4–47, Kelly 2–46, Collins 2–26, Harraway 1–(-2)

#9

Dynasty's Dusk

"This is the time of year I like to study the personnel," Paul Brown told a Cleveland Ad Club luncheon the week before the 1955 NFL Championship. "The good ones get better when the going gets tougher."

Incredibly, this would mark the tenth straight year Brown would get the chance to study his personnel under such conditions—a stretch that had delivered four All-American Conference and two NFL titles. To be that strong for such an extended period of time brought an "inevitable touch of wonder bordering on disbelief," Gordon Cobbledick wrote. "It's impossible, things being as they are, for any professional football team to stay on top for a full decade. And yet, there they are."

Whatever happened the day after Christmas when the Browns would take on the Rams in the title game for the third time in six years, it was clear 1956 promised to be a very different season. Many key players had come and gone in the decade the Browns had existed, but Paul Brown's original player—and without question the franchise's most important—would not return in '56. Brown had lured Otto Graham out of retirement four months earlier to rescue the team from disaster when the coach couldn't find an adequate quarterback to replace him. And Graham only enhanced his legacy, whipping himself into playing form in a matter of days and steering the Browns to a 9–2–1 record and an Eastern Conference title. The United Press International named Graham NFL Player of the Year for his efforts. After a dynamite performance in the '54 title game, Graham knew he would need another inspired showing to ensure he would be remembered in the proper light. Once again, the versatile athlete from Waukegan, Illinois, delivered.

The largest crowd in NFL postseason history—87,695—packed into Los Angeles Memorial Coliseum for a Monday-afternoon showdown under sunny California skies, hoping their Rams could pull an upset over Cleveland just as they had four years before. But as clouds moved in and rain showers began, spoiling the postcard-perfect backdrop at kickoff, both the Rams and their fans realized they never had a chance.

With Graham leading the way, the Browns took complete control of the game in the second quarter and surged to a 17–7 halftime lead. Graham connected with Dante Lavelli for a 56-yard scoring pass in the second quarter just after defensive back Don Paul picked off a Norm Van Brocklin pass and returned it sixty-five yards for a touchdown.

Appropriately, the Browns pulled away in the third with a pair of touchdown runs by Graham. "Automatic Otto" rounded out his career with one last scoring pass, a 35-yarder to Ray Renfro in the fourth to make it 38–7. He finished the day tossing for 209 yards (hitting seven different receivers) while throwing for two scores and running for two more. When Brown sent in George Ratterman to replace Graham, the immense crowd rose and roared to honor Graham, offering its biggest cheer of the day.

Somewhat overshadowed by Graham's farewell was an incredible performance by the Cleveland defense, which picked off seven Los Angeles passes, including six of Van Brocklin's, despite losing key linebacker Chuck Noll and lineman Bob Gain to injury early in the contest.

The 38–14 victory marked the Browns' seventh championship in ten years. While the franchise would continue to be successful for another decade and a half, it would never again reach the level it departed as the sun settled into the Pacific Ocean that cool, cloudy afternoon in Los Angeles. One of the most amazing eras in the history of sports had come to a close.

"The underlying reason why we've been on top," Brown had told the Ad Club earlier that week, "is that these are basically high-class people. They've been able to rise to the occasion when things got tough."

After a ten-year run of success that has never been matched in professional football, it's clear no one rose to the occasion better than Otto Graham.

	1	2	3	4	
Browns	3	14	14	7	=38
Rams	0	7	0	7	=14

First Quarter
CLE-Groza 26-yd. FG

Second Quarter

  CLE-Paul 65-yd. INT return (Groza kick)

  LA-Quinlan 67-yd. pass from Van Brocklin (Richter kick)

  CLE-Lavelli 56-yd. pass from Graham (Groza kick)

Third Quarter

  CLE-Graham 15-yd. run (Groza kick)

  CLE-Graham 1-yd. run (Groza kick)

Fourth Quarter

  CLE-Renfro 35-yd. pass from Graham (Groza kick)

  LA-Waller 4-yd. run (Richter kick)

RUSHING

CLE-Modzelewski 13-61, Bassett 11-49, Morrison 11-33, Graham 9-21,
  Jones 1-3, Smith 3-2

LA-Towler 14-64, Waller 11-48, Wade 1-4

PASSING

CLE-Graham 14-25-3-209

LA-Van Brocklin 11-25-6-166, Wade 0-3-1-0

RECEIVING

CLE-Lavelli 3-95, Renfro 2-49, Modzelewski 5-34, Jones 1-11, Brewster 1-9,
  Morrison 1-7, Bassett 1-4

LA-Quinlan 5-116, Waller 3-18, Fears 1-16, Hirsch 1-9, Towler 1-7

BROWNS 56, DETROIT LIONS 10
DECEMBER 26, 1954

Taking Back Lake Erie

As it turned out, the '54 Indians had rescued the '54 Browns from utter disaster—and given them a historic chance for redemption.

As the Tribe was putting the finishing touches on the finest season in American League history, the Browns wobbled out of the starting gate. They dropped two of their first three games in blowouts to Philadelphia and Pittsburgh and, in Week Four, were scheduled to host the two-time defending champion Detroit Lions—who had beaten the Browns three straight times, including in each of the previous two title games. Another defeat here and Cleveland would drop to 1–3, all but eliminated from contention for a fifth straight conference crown.

That's when fate stepped in. A few weeks earlier, the Indians had clinched the pennant and were set to face the New York Giants in the World Series. The first two contests would be played at the Polo Grounds in New York, with the next three at Cleveland Stadium the following weekend. Game Five was slated for Sunday afternoon, when the Browns and Lions were scheduled to play. The Browns and Indians had ironed out a similar scheduling conflict when the 1948 World Series interfered with a Browns home game and Cleveland Stadium hosted Game Five of the 1948 World Series in the afternoon and a Browns-Brooklyn game that night. This time around, the Browns opted to reschedule their game with Detroit for December 19, the Sunday between the end of the regular season and the championship. The decision saved the season.

Though the Tribe was shockingly swept by the Giants and didn't actually need the use of the Stadium that Sunday, the Browns used their week off to turn themselves around. They ripped off eight straight victories to clinch the Eastern Conference crown and set up a third straight title-game clash with Detroit. When the Browns and Lions made up their rescheduled contest, there was nothing at stake, and both teams played things close to the vest in a meaningless 14–10 Detroit triumph in the snow—the Lions' fourth straight over Cleveland.

There wasn't any reason to expect things to go differently the following Sunday. The media expectations for a Browns loss became so prevalent that at one point Paul Brown smirked and commented, "They're going to let us play the game, aren't they?"

Even without the impending championship game, that Christmas week was one to remember in Cleveland. On Monday afternoon, after thirty-nine hours of deliberation, a jury found noted Bay Village physician Sam Shepherd guilty of killing his wife the previous summer and sentenced him to life imprisonment. It ended the circus-like sixty-five-day trial, the longest in Cleveland history, which had gained national attention—and still would for years to come.

The case did little to ease Cleveland's collective psyche, already severely bruised by the Indians' inexplicable World Series defeat. And now the Browns were poised to become the first football team to lose three straight championships, further sinking the city into a pool of inferiority and proving that they might actually never figure out how to beat the Detroit Lions.

Instead, the Browns casually took the field on an unseasonably warm, sun-splashed Sunday afternoon and shredded the Lions to pieces.

Things started off quite typically for a Browns-Lions game. First, fullback Bill Bowman ripped off a 50-yard run on Detroit's first play from scrimmage. After the Browns caught a reprieve when Lew Carpenter fumbled on the next play, Otto Graham's first pass was intercepted, leading to a Lions field goal. But the Browns' Billy Reynolds returned the ensuing kickoff forty-six yards into Detroit territory, and moments later, Graham connected with Ray Renfro for a 35-yard scoring pass to give the Browns a lead they would not relinquish. Don Paul then picked off Lions quarterback Bobby Layne and returned it thirty-three yards to set up a short Graham–to–Pete Brewster touchdown to make it 14–3. After Reynolds returned a punt forty-two yards to the Lions twelve yard line, it was 21–3 when Graham scored on a 1-yard plunge on the first play of the second quarter.

The rest of the game followed the same pattern. It was 35–10 at halftime as the Browns defense was smothering Layne. The Cleveland offense, generally given a short field to work with, was incredibly potent. Graham hit Brewster for a 43-yard pass in the opening moments of the third quarter to set up another touchdown, then a Ken Konz interception of Layne preceded a 12-yard scoring run by Fred Morrison. When the Lions mustered one last threat late in the third quarter, driving to the Cleveland ten, defensive end Len Ford picked off Layne to end the threat. "They just beat the hell out of us," a humbled Layne said afterward.

The final was 56–10, and fans relieved at finally having the Lion jinx off their backs tore out onto the field and ripped down the goalposts. They then basked in the glory on the field, singing "Auld Lang Syne" with the Browns marching band and celebrating what to this day still stands as the second-largest margin of victory ever in an NFL title game.

Brown called it the finest football team he'd ever coached on a given day. "The emotional outburst came from within," he said. "No one had to stick a needle in them today. They were ready." Detroit coach Buddy Parker was incredulous. "I saw it," he said, "but still hardly can believe it. It has me dazed."

He wasn't the only one. The Browns scored fifty-six points in one game against the Lions after combining for just thirty-nine in their previous four. Graham, who hadn't thrown a touchdown pass in four career games against the Lions, threw three on this day and ran for three more behind an offensive line that "tore apart the Detroit line as if it had been made of wet paper," *Sports Illustrated* wrote. On the other side of the ball, Layne—who had been the Browns' nemesis for four years—had the worst game of his career, throwing six interceptions against a bloodthirsty Cleveland defense. The Lions also lost three fumbles, two of which led directly to Cleveland touchdowns.

With the second-most lopsided championship-game victory in history, the Browns had unloaded years of pent-up frustration. "It took some of the biggest, brawniest psychiatrists in captivity to do it," explained a *Plain Dealer* editorial, "but that horrible haunted inferiority complex that has darkened every Forest City face was whisked away yesterday. . . . Combined with the Indians' domination of the Yankees this year, the victory restored Cleveland's mental health."

The Browns had shaken their reputation as incapable of winning the big game and proved they could outmuscle their Lake Erie rivals. But more importantly, they'd given the city what it needed most. "Cleveland can look the rest of the world straight in the eye this morning," the *Plain Dealer* reported. "We're the champs again."

	1	2	3	4	
Lions	3	7	0	0	=10
Browns	14	21	14	7	=56

First Quarter
   DET-Walker 36-yd. FG
   CLE-Renfro 35-yd. pass from Graham (Groza kick)
   CLE-Brewster 8-yd. pass from Graham (Groza kick)
Second Quarter
   CLE-Graham 1-yd. run (Groza kick)
   DET-Bowman 5-yd. run (Walker kick)
   CLE-Graham 5-yd. run (Groza kick)
   CLE-Renfro 31-yd. pass from Graham (Groza kick)
Third Quarter
   CLE-Graham 1-yd. run (Groza kick)
   CLE-Morrison 12-yd. run (Groza kick)
Fourth Quarter
   CLE-Hanulak 10-yd. run (Groza kick)

RUSHING
DET-Carpenter 8–64, Bowman 7–61, Walker 3–13, Dublinski 2–11, Layne 7–7, Hoernschemeyer 2–2
CLE-Hanvak 5–44, Graham 9–27, Bassett 8–27, Morrison 10–19, Reynolds 6–16, Jones 3–3, Renfro 3–3, Ratterman 1–2

PASSING
DET-Layne 18–42–6–177, Dublinski 1–2–0–18
CLE-Graham 9–12–2–163

RECEIVING
DET-Dibble 4–63, Girard 5–57, Walker 2–39, Hart 1–19, Carpenter 6–17, Bowman 1–6
CLE-Renfro 5–94, Brewster 2–53, Bassett 1–10, Lavelli 1–6

Heaven or Hollywood

Any other conclusion would have been an immense letdown.

After three months of spine-tingling suspense and frantic finishes, the fate of the Kardiac Kids would be decided on the final play of the final game of the regular season.

But the stage for the climax was actually set the week before. After losing a Week Fifteen game in Minnesota on a desperation Hail Mary pass as time expired, the Browns needed a win in the finale to capture the AFC Central title and secure their first playoff bid in eight years. And they'd have to do it in the unfriendly confines of Cincinnati's Riverfront Stadium, where the Browns' playoff hopes had been dashed in each of the previous two season finales. What's more, a pair of former employees were fueled to spike the Browns' boiler.

Bengals owner Paul Brown had never forgiven Art Modell for firing him eighteen years earlier, while Cincy coach Forrest Gregg was still bitter over being forced out as Browns coach before the 1977 season concluded. Nothing would please both Brown and Gregg more than spoiling the Browns' story-book season. The Bengals, Sam Rutigliano noted, would be "loose as a goose because they don't have anything to lose. But the game means a great deal for us. We have come a long, long way, and we don't intend for it to stop now.

"This is the way it should be. If we're not good enough to beat the Bengals, we don't deserve to be in the playoffs."

Though Cincinnati stood at just 6–9, it had won three straight and was already building momentum for what would become a Super Bowl season in 1981. Parlaying that progress, the Bengals surged to a 10–0 first-quarter lead over the hesitant Browns, and the Riverfront crowd roared. The physical tone of the contest was set early when Thom Darden drilled Cincy wideout Pat

McInally over the middle with a shot to the head that knocked him out of the game. McInally would return, but the rough theme would only continue.

As they had all year, the Browns surged back. Brian Sipe hit Reggie Rucker for a long touchdown pass, then Don Cockroft tied the contest with a field goal fourteen seconds before the half. As the teams began the second half, the Browns were playing well and on the brink of taking control of the contest. But on the second play of what would become a wild third quarter, Cincinnati cornerback Ray Griffin intercepted Sipe and returned the football fifty-two yards for the go-ahead touchdown. The Browns had dug themselves another hole. "After Griffin ran it back, I felt more aggressive than I had at any time in the game," Sipe said, "and I was determined that they wouldn't beat us."

Once again, the Browns responded. Fueled by motivation to atone for his miscue, Sipe caught fire. He connected with sparingly used receiver Ricky Feacher for back-to-back touchdown passes from thirty-five and thirty-four yards to catapult the Browns back into the lead. But on the final play of the third quarter, McInally earned his revenge, reeling in a 59-yard touchdown pass from Jack Thompson to knot the game at twenty-four.

The final fifteen minutes were among the most brutal, most competitive in Browns history. Both defenses rose to the occasion, not permitting the game-breaking play. When the Bengals drove to the Cleveland twenty yard line with eight minutes left, Darden picked off Thompson to halt the march. But a play later, Ken Riley returned the favor, intercepting Sipe at the Cincinnati thirty-four. Then the Browns caught the tide-turning break when McInally shanked a 15-yard punt that gave the Browns a first down at their forty-five with 6:04 left.

"Look," Sipe told his teammates in the huddle, "if we're going to be champs, we've got to do it now. We've got to control the ball and get some points. This is it." Though the Cleveland offense had ridden Sipe's arm all season, it was Mike Pruitt who sparked the final drive. Pruitt carried the football five times for thirty-one yards, pushing the Browns slowly but steadily into Cincinnati territory and setting up a 22-yard field goal by Don Cockroft with 1:25 to play. The Browns led, 27–24, but the game was far from over. The script would have a perfect ending. If the Browns could hold, they belonged in the playoffs. If not, they didn't.

Gregg decided to replace Thompson with injured veteran Ken Anderson for the final possession, and Anderson guided Cincinnati into Cleveland territory with eleven seconds left. Out of time-outs at the Cleveland thirty-four yard line, the Bengals needed one more first down to claw within field-goal range. Anderson hit Steve Kreider angling toward the sideline at the Cleveland thirteen, but Ron Bolton smashed the tight end before he could get out of bounds to stop the clock. After the final four seconds finally ticked down, the Browns were division champions for the first time in nine years on the strength of one of the most dramatic victories in team history. "Scripted in heaven or Hollywood," Jim Braham wrote in the *Cleveland Press,* "what other ending would have fit Cleveland's 'Kardiac Kids'?"

Rutigliano was hoisted on the shoulders of Rucker and Lyle Alzado and carried off the field as the massive celebration began. When the Browns arrived back in Cleveland that evening, 18,000 fans were waiting to cheer them despite an 11-degree temperature. Among them was Cleveland mayor George Voinovich. "This is the best thing that's happened to the city since I've been mayor, next to getting out of default," Voinovich said. "But maybe this is more important."

"On the way they have learned some lessons," Hal Lebovitz wrote. "And they have learned about themselves. They have what it takes. They're champions. That's happiness."

	1	2	3	4	
Browns	0	10	14	3	=27
Bengals	3	7	14	0	=24

First Quarter
   CIN-Breech 42-yd. FG
Second Quarter
   CIN-Thompson 13-yd. run (Breech kick)
   CLE-Rucker 42-yd. pass from Sipe (Cockroft kick)
   CLE-Cockroft 26-yd. FG
Third Quarter
   CIN-R. Griffin 52-yd. INT return (Breech kick)
   CLE-Feacher 35-yd. pass from Sipe (Cockroft kick)
   CLE-Feacher 34-yd. pass from Sipe (Cockroft kick)
   CIN-McInally 59-yd. pass from Thompson (Breech kick)
Fourth Quarter
   CLE-Cockroft 22-yd. FG

RUSHING
CLE-M. Pruitt 14–51, Miller 3–7, G. Pruitt 1–2, Sipe 1–(-3)
CIN-Alexander 8–50, Johnson 16–42, Thompson 4–30, A. Griffin 2–3, Harris 1–0

PASSING

CLE-Sipe 24–44–2–308

CIN-Thompson 12–30–2–197, Anderson 4–6–0–54

RECEIVING

CLE-Rucker 4–74, Feacher 2–69, Logan 1–65, Newsome 5–30, Adams 1–26, Hill 2–16, M. Pruitt 6–11, G. Pruitt 2–10, Miller 1–7

CIN-McInally 3–86, Ross 5–77, Kreider 3–54, Curtis 2–17, Harris 1–7, Alexander 1–5, A. Griffin 1–5

#6

DENVER BRONCOS 23, BROWNS 20 (OT)
JANUARY 11, 1987

A Slow Death

It was supposed to be a coronation.

After nearly two decades of heartbreak and frustration, the Cleveland Browns were on the brink of their first Super Bowl appearance. They'd already proven themselves as a team of destiny in 1986, roaring to a 12–4 regular-season mark, then pulling off a remarkable comeback to win their divisional playoff against New York, the franchise's first postseason victory in seventeen years. The Pandemonium Palace that was Cleveland Stadium would be filled to the rafters with crazed fans who'd been waiting their entire lives for this moment. History was about to be made, and Cleveland was about to shake the entire world off its back. "I see a Browns team that simply does not believe it can be beaten," Bill Livingston wrote in the *Plain Dealer*.

All that stood in the Browns' way was a team from the foothills of the Rocky Mountains, wearing construction-barrel orange jerseys—and its quarterback.

The city of Cleveland was already punch-drunk in love with its Browns before they'd reached the AFC Championship, but in the week leading up to what would become an epic confrontation with the Denver Broncos, Northeast Ohio nearly imploded with civic joy. Bridal shops added specials on brown-and-orange gowns. Radio stations buzzed with adapted songs about the Browns' heroics. A huge "Go Browns" banner was wrapped around the control tower at Hopkins Airport. "It was an amazing time to see the city," nose tackle and Cleveland native Bob Golic said. "From the time we got up in the morning to the time we went to bed at night, it was all about us."

Wired from well before the opening kickoff, the fans were given plenty to cheer about in the early going. On their second possession, the Browns marched eighty-six yards and surged into the lead when versatile running back Herman Fontenot took a swing pass from Kosar on third-and-goal from the Denver six and snuck across the goal line for the game's first score. With rocket-armed Bronco quarterback John Elway tamed by the Cleveland defense, the Browns were poised to take control of the game.

But just when the opportunity presented itself, the Browns began shooting themselves in their collective foot. They committed three turnovers in a stretch of five offensive plays, allowing Denver to creep to a 10–7 advantage. Cleveland tied the contest at intermission, and the defenses slugged it out through most of the second half. The score was 13–13 when the Browns reached midfield with just under six minutes to play.

With tension mounting, Kosar dropped back on third-and-six from the Denver forty-eight yard line and flung a long pass for his most reliable receiver, Brian Brennan, streaking down the left sideline. Brennan turned Denver safety Dennis Smith inside out, caught the pass at the eighteen and scampered into the end zone for the touchdown that appeared destined to send the Browns to Super Bowl XXI. "I was literally shaking," Brennan said, "having caught the pass that was going to propel us to the Super Bowl." And things would only get better.

Denver's Gene Lang misplayed the ensuing kickoff from Cleveland kicker Mark Moseley, and the Broncos wound up taking over at their own two yard line with 5:34 left. With the Stadium crowd going bonkers and the Lamar Hunt Trophy already being wheeled into the Browns locker room, the celebration had begun. But John Elway didn't play along.

Already considered a disappointment by some after entering the NFL with colossal expectations, Elway had proven himself dangerous, though inconsistent and perhaps a bit immature in his first four seasons in the NFL. In the next five minutes, however, he would surpass all aspirations.

Things started innocently enough. The Broncos dug themselves out from their hole and eked out a pair of first downs. They had only reached their own twenty-six yard line in a little over three minutes, though. Needing a touchdown to tie, they'd have to pick up the pace, and Elway did, first hitting Steve Sewell over the middle for twenty-two yards, then firing a 20-yard strike to rookie wideout Mark Jackson, which wiped out a critical third-and-eighteen situation. "It was like somebody was shooting you in the shoulder, then in the right forearm, then in the left foot," Brennan said. "It was like a slow death."

With the Stadium crowd becoming more subdued with each play, the Broncos reached the Cleveland five yard line, where, on third-and-goal, the inevitable happened. Elway fired another rifle shot for Jackson, who caught it rolling in the end zone for the game-tying touchdown with thirty-seven seconds left.

Many football fans—and many Browns fans, for that matter—remember little from the overtime session that followed. The Browns won the coin toss and took over at their own thirty. Facing third-and-two two plays later, Fontenot was wrapped up for no gain on a peculiar sweep play call, and the Browns were forced to punt. They never saw the ball again. Taking over at his own twenty-five yard line, Elway completed a remarkable 27-yard third-down pass on the run to Steve Watson that pushed Denver into field-goal range.

Moments later, Salem, Ohio, native Rich Karlis was called upon for a 33-yard kick that wafted up over the left goalpost and appeared to many to be a miss. But the officials ruled the kick good, and the Broncos were Super Bowl–bound. "Thank God they don't have instant replays on field goals," Karlis would say.

The Browns and their fans were absolutely stunned. "It was like my heart dropped out of my chest," Golic said. The only sound in the Stadium was the whooping of the triumphant Denver players. "There's dead silence for about a minute," Browns center Mike Baab said. "And as we walked off the field to go to the dugout, one guy started clapping. Then another guy started clapping. And then 100 people started clapping. And the next thing you know, the whole Stadium stood up and gave us this roaring, incredible standing ovation that lasted ten or fifteen minutes.

"They were thanking us for being the best God-damned Browns team they'd ever had."

And for providing one of the most dramatic games in NFL history—even if it didn't have a happy ending.

	1	2	3	4	OT	
Broncos	0	10	3	7	3	=23
Browns	7	3	0	10	0	=20

First Quarter
  CLE-Fontenot 6-yd. pass from Kosar (Moseley kick)
Second Quarter
  DEN-Karlis 19-yd. FG
  DEN-Wilhite 1-yd. run (Karlis kick)
  CLE-Moseley 29-yd. FG
Third Quarter
  DEN-Karlis 26-yd. FG
Fourth Quarter
  CLE-Moseley 25-yd. FG
  CLE-Brennan 48-yd. pass from Kosar (Moseley kick)
  DEN-Jackson 5-yd. pass from Elway (Karlis kick)

Overtime
   DEN-Karlis 33-yd. FG

RUSHING
DEN-Winder 26–83, Elway 4–56, Lang 3–9, Sewell 1–1, Wilhite 3–0
CLE-Mack 26–94, Kosar 4–3, Fontenot 3–3

PASSING
DEN-Elway 22–38–1–244
CLE-Kosar 18–32–2–259

RECEIVING
DEN-Watson 3–55, Sewell 3–47, Mobley 3–36, Johnson 3–25, Jackson 2–25,
   Kay 2–23, Wilhite 2–20, Sampson 1–10, Winder 2–2, Lang 1–1
CLE-Brennan 4–72, Fontenot 7–66, Weathers 1–42, Langhorne 2–35, Mack
   2–20, Slaughter 1–20, Byner 1–4

Straight from the Heart

For three years, while much of the media focused on the heroics of Bernie Kosar, Marty Schottenheimer consistently pointed out that while Kosar may have been the catalyst to the Browns' run of success in the 1980s, he wasn't the heart of the team. That title belonged to Earnest Byner, who had progressed from an unknown tenth-round draft choice to one of the most versatile offensive weapons in football.

When the Browns fell to the Denver Broncos in the 1986 AFC Championship, many Cleveland backers were quick to point out that because he'd missed half the season to an injury, Byner was not a factor—and consequently he might have been *the* factor. A year later, he'd get that chance.

As the bizarre 1987 season unfolded, the Browns and their fans wanted nothing more than another shot at Denver, to dish out some payback for their playoff defeat the previous January. A highly anticipated Monday-night duel between the teams in September was wiped out due to a players' strike, but the teams' destinies would prove intertwined again. After both the Browns and Broncos won their respective divisions and coasted to divisional-playoff triumphs, they would once again meet for the conference crown, this time in Denver's Mile High Stadium.

Cleveland players, coaches, and fans alike felt the '87 Browns were even stronger than the '86 team and would stand a better chance to reach the Super Bowl. But in the first thirty minutes of the rematch, the Browns did everything in their power to punch the Broncos' Super Bowl ticket.

Turnovers on Cleveland's first two possessions led to a pair of quick Denver touchdowns. Picking up where he'd left off the year before, John Elway carved through the Browns defense for another score midway through the second quarter, and the Broncos took a stunning 21–3 lead into the locker room at halftime. The Browns came out relaxed and focused in the third quarter and quickly scored on a Kosar–to–Reggie Langhorne pass, but then Elway worked his magic again. He somehow eluded a heavy Browns pass rush and turned a broken third-down play into an 80-yard touchdown pass that gave Denver a seemingly insurmountable 28–10 lead five minutes into the second half.

With many fans from coast to coast flicking off their television sets, and the party already begun at Mile High, the Browns—sparked by Kosar and Byner— refused to surrender. The Cleveland offense caught fire, ripping off touchdowns on four consecutive possessions as Kosar completed eleven of thirteen passes for 188 yards and three touchdowns in just over a quarter of play. Byner caught three of those passes for ninety-seven yards, including a 33-yard touchdown and a picture-perfect 53-yard third-down reception. When Kosar slung a key third-down pass to Webster Slaughter for a 5-yard touchdown with 10:45 remaining, they'd come all the way back to force a 31–31 tie. "They were running like a machine," Denver linebacker Ricky Hunley said. "Every play they ran was executed perfectly." The stage was set for a remarkable conclusion.

After holding Elway and the Broncos in check throughout the second half, the Browns defense finally yielded. Denver's Golden Boy hit two long completions, then running back Sammy Winder turned a simple dump-off screen pass into a 20-yard touchdown to give the home team the lead again, 38–31.

Kosar and the Browns offense took over at their own twenty-four yard line with 3:53 remaining—essentially mirroring the situation of the finale of the previous year's AFC Championship, only with the roles reversed. Byner sprinted up the middle for seventeen yards. Kosar hit Brian Brennan for thirteen, then twenty yards, pushing the Browns into Denver territory at the two-minute warning. A Denver penalty followed another Byner run, and the Browns were at the Bronco eight yard line with just over a minute to play. With the Denver defense on its heels, the Browns were poised to tie the game and take a tidal wave of momentum into sudden death.

The play call on second-and-goal was "13-Trap," a misdirected handoff to Byner that unfolded exactly as it had been drawn up. Byner, who had served as the team's emotional center for so long, burst inside the five and was destined to score. But an obscure defensive back named Jeremiah Castille blindsided Byner at the three, and Byner dropped the football. A huge pileup ensued, and the Broncos recovered.

The Browns and their fans across the nation were paralyzed with shock. For the second straight year, the Browns had been on the cusp of a Super Bowl berth only to see it slip away in the cruelest of fashions. This time around, the pain was even greater, and the heartbreak would haunt the franchise for decades to come. "Not many people get a second chance in life," said Ozzie Newsome. "We did, and we didn't win. That makes this loss twice as frustrating as last year."

"I've been involved with a lot of teams and a lot of players in my years in this game," Schottenheimer said afterward, his voice quivering, "but I've never been more proud of a group of men than I am today of that group, the Cleveland Browns."

Byner, an instant goat in the eyes of the sports world, saw the achievements of his career afternoon evaporate. He'd caught seven passes for 120 yards and rushed for 67 more, scoring a pair of touchdowns. It was simply the continuation of a mind-boggling trend. In the three career postseason games he'd played at full strength, Byner rushed for 350 yards, reeled in 181 in receptions, and scored six touchdowns. "Byner symbolizes that great fighting spirit," wrote Cleveland radio personality Pete Franklin. "He is the guy who refuses to give up, who keeps on battling the opponent."

"There was something very Cleveland-like in the way Byner, knowing he already had the first down, strove to make it in the end zone." Doug Clarke wrote. "Disappointed, yes; bitter and angry, no. How do you get mad at a team that refused to quit and provided us with one of the most thrilling of championship games in the history of the NFL?"

"If it had been anybody in the world but Earnest, we would have killed him," Mike Baab would say. "But without Earnest, we never would have gotten there. Earnest was that kind of person. He was a team leader, and we all knew Earnest came straight from the heart."

And when Byner was casually traded away a year later as an indirect result of pro football's most infamous turnover, the Browns lost *their* heart.

	1	2	3	4	
Browns	0	3	21	9	=33
Broncos	14	7	10	7	=38

First Quarter
    DEN-Nattiel 8-yd. pass from Elway (Karlis kick)
    DEN-Sewell 2-yd. run (Karlis kick)
Second Quarter
    CLE-Bahr 24-yd. FG
    DEN-Lang 1-yd. run (Karlis kick)

Third Quarter
CLE-Langhorne 18-yd. pass from Kosar (Bahr kick)
DEN-Jackson 80-yd. pass from Elway (Karlis kick)
CLE-Byner 33-yd. pass from Kosar (Bahr kick)
CLE-Byner 4-yd. run (Bahr kick)
DEN-Karlis 38-yd. FG
Fourth Quarter
CLE-Slaughter 5-yd. pass from Kosar (Bahr kick)
DEN-Winder 20-yd. pass from Elway (Karlis kick)
CLE-Safety: Horan ran out of end zone

RUSHING
CLE-Byner 15–67, Mack 12–61
DEN-Winder 20–72, Lang 5–51, Elway 11–36, Sewell 1–1, Boddie 1–8, Horan 1–(-12)

PASSING
CLE-Kosar 26–41–1–356
DEN-Elway 14–26–1–281

RECEIVING
CLE-Byner 7–120, Slaughter 4–53, Brennan 4–48, Langhorne 2–48, Newsome 3–35, Mack 4–28, Weathers 1–19, Tennell 1–5
DEN-Jackson 4–134, Nattiel 5–95, Winder 3–34, Sewell 1–10, Mobley 1–8

BROWNS 35, PHILADELPHIA EAGLES 10
SEPTEMBER 16, 1950

The World Series of Football

When the All-American Football Conference was founded in 1944, founder Arch Ward envisioned a day when the AAFC and NFL would be like baseball's American and National leagues—each sending its champion to face the other in a World Series of professional football.

It never happened. Despite constructing a handful of strong teams, the AAFC was predominately disregarded by the NFL in its four-year existence. Ironically, after the All-American Conference folded following the 1949 season, Ward's dream came true.

The Browns, four-time champions and cream of the AAFC crop, were enveloped into the NFL along with the San Francisco 49ers and Baltimore Colts. League schedule-makers smelled money and saw a perfect opportunity for the opening game of the 1950 season. They paired the Browns with the two-time NFL-champion Philadelphia Eagles, considered by many to be the greatest team of all time. And with thirty-one of the thirty-two players from the '49 title team returning, the consensus was simple: the Eagles would crush these untested newcomers.

Philly's strength was its defense, which had permitted just 134 points in all of 1949—an average of just over eleven per contest. Eagles coach Greasy Neale insisted his squad needn't even scout the Browns or watch any films on them. The Browns were strictly a good passing team, Neale insisted, and once the Eagles took that away, Cleveland would fold. "I presume," Paul Brown offered with his trademark dry wit, "we've won our last football game."

More than 70,000 fans packed into Philadelphia's Municipal Stadium on a warm Saturday night to see their defending champions prove their dominance once again. Yet things started ominously. The Eagles were forced to punt after three plays on their first possession, and the Browns' Don Phelps returned the kick sixty-four yards for a touchdown. It was brought back on an illegal block—which Paul Brown insisted was a phantom call—but the tone had been set.

After the Eagles snuck to a 3–0 advantage, Otto Graham hit Dub Jones for a 59-yard score, the Browns' first touchdown in the NFL. The Eagles then had a perfect opportunity to take the lead back after recovering a Marion Motley fumble in Cleveland territory and marching to the Browns three yard line. But Motley, inserted at linebacker, atoned for his miscue by making three straight tackles to keep the Eagles from scoring.

A Cliff Lewis interception led to another Cleveland touchdown, this one a 26-yard Graham–to–Dante Lavelli strike that made it 14–3 at the half. Any hopes of a Philly comeback were snuffed out in the opening moments of the third quarter when Graham hit on five straight passes, setting up a 12-yard scoring toss to Mac Speedie and a 21–3 lead. Interestingly, the Eagles started the drive double-covering both Speedie and Lavelli, but Graham adjusted and picked the Philadelphia defense apart with passes to halfbacks Jones and Rex Bumgardner. The Eagles quickly abandoned the strategy, and then Graham hit Speedie for the score.

As the third quarter progressed, Brown called up to offensive coach Blanton Collier in the press box. "What are they doing now?" Brown asked. "How are they covering our receivers?" Collier thought about it for a moment. "Truthfully," he said, "I don't know. I can't tell because I'm sure they don't know what they're trying to do themselves."

The greatest team in the history of football had met its match. The final was 35–10, as the Browns simply exploded into the NFL. "At the finish the National League champions were weary and disappointed and physically beaten," wrote Gordon Cobbledick. "But mostly they were just plain bewildered. They had been hit from more angles than they knew existed."

This bewilderment was reflected by the control tower at the airport when the Browns took off to return to Cleveland the following morning. "The field is clear," the tower reported to the pilot. "Take off and get those Browns out of Philadelphia."

"Jeez," a humbled Neale said after the game, "they've got a lotta guns, haven't they? A lotta guns."

The most lethal weapon was Graham, who completed twenty-one passes for 346 yards and three touchdowns, while rushing for another. "Graham is the ideal passer," Neale admitted. "He just hangs the ball up there and lets the receivers go and get it. I've been trying to get our passers to throw that way for ten years, but they haven't got the knack." The Browns' offensive success didn't come solely through the air, though. They also racked up 141 rushing yards on twenty-four carries for an average of nearly six yards per rush. Philadelphia's mighty running game only accumulated 148 yards on forty-four attempts, barely three yards per carry.

In the course of one September night in Philadelphia, the world of professional football had changed forever. NFL Commissioner Bert Bell visited the Cleveland locker room after the game and called the Browns "the best football team I have ever seen." Browns guard Lin Houston admitted, "I had never seen perfection until that game, or after that game. But in that game, it was perfection." Brown would call it the most emotional game he ever coached. "We had four years of constant ridicule to get us ready," he said.

When Eagles wide receiver Pete Pihos, who had scored his team's only touchdown in the fourth quarter, met his wife after the game, she asked what had happened to his mighty Eagles. "It's all right honey," Pihos replied. "We just met up with a team from the big league."

	1	2	3	4	
Browns	7	7	7	14	=35
Eagles	3	0	0	7	=10

First Quarter
PHI-Patton 15-yd. FG
CLE-D. Jones 59-yd. pass from Graham (Grigg kick)
Second Quarter
CLE-Lavelli 26-yd. pass from Graham (Grigg kick)
Third Quarter
CLE-Speedie 12-yd. pass from Graham (Grigg kick)
Fourth Quarter
PHI-Pihos 17-yd. pass from Mackrides (Patton kick)
CLE-Graham 1-yd. run (Grigg kick)
CLE-Bumgardner 1-yd. run (Grigg kick)

Rushing
CLE-D. Jones 6–72, Motley 11–48, Bumgardner 4–18, Graham 4–3
PHI-Ziegler 17–57, Scott 13–46, Craft 4–28, Myers 5–12, Mackrides 2–2, Pavmer 2–2, Thompson 1–1

PASSING
CLE-Graham 21–38–2–346
PHI-Thompson 8–24–2–73, Mackrides 3–8–1–45

RECEIVING
CLE-Speedie 7–109, D. Jones 5–98, Lavelli 4–76, Bumgardner 3–27, Motley
    2–26
PHI-Pinos 4–51, Myers 2–29, Ferrante 3–24, Ziegler 2–14.

BROWNS 23, NEW YORK JETS 20 (2 OT)
JANUARY 3, 1987

Back from the Dead

They were two teams headed in dramatically opposite directions.

In November, the 1986 Browns had caught fire, winning their last five games and eight of their last nine. With young Bernie Kosar developing rapidly each week, the Browns offense kept getting better, while the defense overcame an early-season slump and now resembled the dominant force it had become two years prior.

Meanwhile, by the beginning of December, the New York Jets were in shambles. After rocketing to a dazzling 10–1 start, the Jets lost the last five games of the regular season, tumbled out of first place in the AFC East, and backed into the playoffs as a Wild Card team. They'd put it together in a blowout victory over Kansas City in the Wild Card Game, but there was little doubt they'd once again crash and burn against the red-hot Browns, who seemed destined for a trip to Super Bowl XXI.

Early on, though, the Jets looked like anything but seven-point underdogs. A flea-flicker touchdown pass from Pat Ryan to Wesley Walker gave New York a 7–0 lead, but the Browns countered with a long Kosar–to–Herman Fontenot scoring aerial. Though the teams were tied at ten entering the second half, the upstart Jets were having the better of play.

The once-mighty New York defense, led by loudmouth lineman Mark Gastineau, had returned to form and was thwarting Kosar and Co. The frustration appeared to peak early in the fourth quarter when the Browns, trailing 13–10, drove to the New York two yard line, only to have a third-down Kosar pass picked off in the end zone. Things would get even worse.

After regaining possession at his own seventeen yard line with 4:31 left, Kosar made another crucial mistake. On first down, he was intercepted again, and the Jets suddenly had victory in their grasp. On the next snap, running back Freeman McNeil sprinted through the line and angled into the end zone for a 25-yard scoring run that made it 20–10 with 4:14 remaining.

The sellout crowd, which had shook the foundation of Cleveland Stadium prior to kickoff, was deathly silent. Their team of destiny was about to make a stunning early exit from the playoffs.

Even worse, the bumbling Cleveland offense continued to fizzle. Three plays after taking over, the Browns faced second-and-twenty-four at the seventeen, and then a Kosar pass fell incomplete. But the flamboyant Gastineau, who had spent much of the possession taunting Cleveland fans in the bleachers, drilled Kosar late and was penalized for roughing the passer, giving the Browns an automatic first down—and new life.

As if flicking a switch, Kosar awoke. "I saw a look in his eyes I'd never seen before," Ozzie Newsome said. "He was not going to be denied." Cleveland's hometown hero completed five passes and drove the Browns to the New York one yard line, where Kevin Mack scored to cut the deficit to 20–17 with 1:57 left. The Jets put another nail in the Cleveland coffin by recovering the ensuing onside kick, but the Browns defense quickly overwhelmed New York and forced a punt. Kosar and the offense regained possession at the Cleveland thirty-two with fifty-three seconds left and no time-outs.

After a pass-interference penalty on the Jets pushed the Browns to the New York forty-two yard line, Kosar launched a rifle shot down the left sideline that Webster Slaughter reeled in at the Jets five. What was left of the Stadium crowd exploded in surprise and joy. "I remember the feeling of, 'Oh my God, we're doing this,'" Bob Golic said. After inadvertently melting twenty-four seconds off the clock because they thought Slaughter had gone out of bounds after the play, the Browns hurriedly stopped the clock with fifteen seconds showing. Veteran kicker Mark Moseley, who had been picked up by Cleveland the month before when Matt Bahr was lost to a knee injury, booted a 22-yard field goal with seven seconds left to tie the contest and force overtime. Thousands of fans who shortly before had left angry and disappointed reversed their direction and returned to the stadium for overtime.

The Jets won the toss but were once again annihilated by the Cleveland defense and forced to punt. Kosar then picked up right where he left off, connecting on three short passes and hitting Reggie Langhorne for a 35-yard gain to the Jets five yard line. Marty Schottenheimer, who had been the Browns defensive coordinator during "Red Right 88," wasted no time. He sent out Moseley to win the game then and there with a chip-shot 23-yard field goal.

Inexplicably, Moseley missed it badly wide right, and now it was the Jets who had received a stay of execution. The game marched on.

The teams battled through the remainder of the overtime period and continued into a second. The Cleveland defense continued to dominate, limiting the Jets to just one first down and twelve total yards on three overtime possessions. "I've never seen the kind of push and penetration from a defensive line that we had in overtime," Schottenheimer said later. It was already the third-longest game in NFL history when the Browns finally got another drive going. Behind the power running of Mack, they marched to the New York nine yard line, and Schottenheimer once again called on Moseley, who felt every ounce of pressure. "It was as if 80,000 people were riding on my shoulders," he said, "every one of them with a knife behind his back." But this time, at the opposite end of the field, the curly-haired thirty-eight-year-old kicker didn't disappoint. With patches of sunlight filtering through the ashen January sky for the first time since kickoff, Moseley calmly connected on a 27-yard field goal. After four hours and eleven minutes of tension, the city of Cleveland lapsed into unparalleled bedlam. The celebration that unfolded in downtown Cleveland that evening was like "the biggest wedding you've ever been to combined with New Year's Eve and the end of the war," the *Plain Dealer* described.

So overcome with jubilation, many Browns fans didn't realize the historical significance of what they'd just witnessed. It was Cleveland's first postseason victory in seventeen years and because of it, the Browns would make their first-ever appearance in the AFC Championship Game. Only the epic 1971 Miami–Kansas City playoff and the 1962 AFL Championship were longer contests. Kosar, who had been flustered for much of the afternoon, rewrote the NFL playoff record book by completing thirty-three of sixty-four passes for 489 yards.

"I think we all had an opportunity to experience one of the finest games in the history of the sport," Schottenheimer said. "I have never experienced or seen a comeback like that. After it was over, just before we said our prayer in the locker room, I told the players to listen. You could still hear the people cheering for us.

"This is a victory, a game, a moment all of us will remember the rest of our lives."

	1	2	3	4	OT	2OT	
Jets	7	3	3	7	0	0	=20
Browns	7	3	0	10	0	3	=23

First Quarter
   NY-Walker 42-yd. pass from Ryan (Leahy kick)
   CLE-Fontenot 37-yd. pass from Kosar (Moseley kick)
Second Quarter
   CLE-Moseley 39-yd. FG
   NY-Leahy 46-yd. FG
Third Quarter
   NY-Leahy 38-yd. FG
Fourth Quarter
   NY-McNeil 25-yd. run (Leahy kick)
   CLE-Mack 1-yd. run (Moseley kick)
   CLE-Moseley 22-yd. FG
Second Overtime
   CLE-Moseley 27-yd. FG

RUSHING
NY-McNeil 25–71, O'Brien 3–22, Paige 3–11
CLE-Mack 20–63, Fontenot 3–8, Dickey 3–4, Kosar 1–0

PASSING
NY-O'Brien 11–19–0–134, Ryan 6–11–0–103
CLE-Kosar 33–64–2–489, Brennan 1–1–0–5

RECEIVING
NY-Toon 5–93, Walker 2–49, Shuler 4–43, McNeil 4–35, Sohn 1–7, Paige
   1–10
CLE-Newsome 6–114, Slaughter 6–86, Brennan 4–69, Langhorne 4–65, Fontenot 5–62, Mack 5–51, Holt 2–42, Weathers 1–3, Dickey 1–2

Out of the Blue

As Chuck Heaton performed an informal survey among Cleveland Christmas shoppers, his assumption was validated: there was a decided note of pessimism concerning the Browns' upcoming appearance in the NFL title game. Though it would be Cleveland's first championship appearance in seven years, no one thought the Browns stood a chance against the mighty Baltimore Colts. "There seems to be a feeling about town that young Don Shula has assembled a squad of supermen," Heaton wrote. "They are believed to be capable of running the Browns right into Lake Erie."

There really didn't seem to be much point in playing the game, which appeared would be little more than a coronation for the mighty Colts. Boasting the league's finest defense, the Colts had gone 12–2 in 1964, allowing just over sixteen points per contest. They also scored 428 themselves—becoming the third-highest scoring team in NFL history as they coasted to the Western Conference title. In a glowing feature that October, *Sports Illustrated* had already labeled the Colts the NFL's new dynasty. "To be realistic about it," *SI*'s Edwin Shrake wrote that week prior to the title game, "the championship game of 1964 has already been played. Baltimore won it in October by beating Green Bay for the second time."

The Browns, on the other hand, had slumped near season's end, nearly blowing a comfortable lead in the East and saving it only with a blowout victory over the miserable New York Giants in the finale. The Cleveland offense, led by Jim Brown and a precise passing attack, was one of the league's strongest, but the defense had not had a particularly good year, permitting nearly 300 points in fourteen games while allowing more yards than any team in the NFL.

Naturally, the Colts were seven-point favorites despite having to play on the road, but both the home team and its fans were hopeful. "I feel good about going into this game," Browns defensive back Bernie Parrish said that week. "I believe we'll beat the Colts and that our defense will give a good account for itself." Heaton went against the national trend, picking the Browns to win while noting it was "based on more than hunch and hope."

Better than 79,000 fans—the second-largest championship crowd in league history—would pack into Cleveland Stadium on a cold, raw Sunday afternoon, while thousands of others scampered out of town to watch the game on television. With league blackout rules not allowing CBS's broadcast of the game in the Cleveland area, fans reserved hotel rooms with television sets in nearby cities like Erie and Toledo to be sure they would see whatever happened. And they would be glad they did.

Rather than dominating the Browns in the early going, the Colts could simply match Cleveland as the teams fought through a rugged, scoreless first half. Baltimore had just one substantial drive to the Cleveland nineteen yard line early in the second but came away with nothing when a field-goal attempt went awry on a bad snap. With the wind gusting up to thirty miles per hour, both passing attacks stalled, and Frank Ryan would later call it the worst wind he'd ever played in. But with the wind at their backs in the third quarter, the Browns began perhaps the finest half of football in team history.

After forcing a Colt punt, the Browns finally put a decent drive together and took the lead on a Lou Groza field goal. The Cleveland defense rose up again, forcing another punt, and then Jim Brown took center stage. Still looking for his first championship, Brown took a sweep around left end in the double-wing formation and wove down the frozen field for a stunning 46-yard gain that opened the floodgates. On the next play, Ryan threaded a pass through the goalposts to Gary Collins for an 18-yard touchdown, and suddenly, the Browns were up 10–0.

The script continued: another Baltimore punt, another Collins touchdown. This one was good for forty-two yards as Collins broke wide open over the middle and reeled in the pass to make it 17–0. The sellout crowd was ecstatic, and hotel rooms from Northwest Ohio to upstate New York echoed in celebration. Things would only get better: another Groza field goal made the lead twenty points, and then Collins capped the finest day of his career. He made a remarkable catch of another long Ryan pass despite good coverage from Baltimore defensive back Bobby Boyd, then plowed into the end zone for a 51-yard touchdown to make the final 27–0. In addition to his record-breaking three touchdowns, Collins racked up 130 yards on five receptions and was named *Sport Magazine*'s MVP, for which he was given a new Corvette.

In the final seconds, well over a thousand fans rushed onto the field and tore down both sets of goalposts, mauling the Cleveland players in jubilation. The "experts" in the press box looked at one another in stunned silence and shook their heads "after what well may be the best performance ever in the sparkling history of this football club," Heaton wrote. "This was a Browns team that decided it would prove something." The Baltimore offense that was supposed to roll up thirty-plus points was held to a harmless 171 total yards, as the Cleveland defensive line pressured Johnny Unitas all afternoon, limiting him to just twelve completions and forcing a pair of interceptions. *Sports Illustrated,* which had already placed the crown on the Colts' heads, admitted, "The Browns suddenly became one of the great defensive teams in championship-game history." Accordingly, the magazine had planned a splashy color layout of Unitas on the cover of its next issue. But when the Browns didn't cooperate, *SI* had to scramble and stick a black-and-white action shot of Frank Ryan on the cover.

As the team gathered for a formal celebration at the Hotel Sheraton, fans packed into downtown bars to toast the new champions. "Every citizen of Greater Cleveland today can feel a little happier, a little more elated," read a *Plain Dealer* editorial. "There's no civic advertisement that's quite the same as 'Home of the Champions.'"

"Nothing—no manifestation of Nature, no machination of Man—could stand in the way yesterday of the Cleveland Browns," the *PD*'s Dan Robertson wrote. "And now they are the football champions of the world. And but good."

As the celebration carried into the frosty December night, no one could have predicted it would be the last party of its kind in Cleveland for generations to come. "Cleveland won't forget it for a long, long time," the *Plain Dealer* editorial declared.

Nobody had any idea just how telling those words would become.

	1	2	3	4	
Colts	0	0	0	0	= 0
Browns	0	0	17	10	=27

Third Quarter
    CLE-Groza 43-yd. FG
    CLE-Collins 18-yd. pass from Ryan (Groza kick)
    CLE-Collins 42-yd. pass from Ryan (Groza kick)
Fourth Quarter
    CLE-Groza 9-yd. FG
    CLE-Collins 51-yd. pass from Ryan (Groza kick)

RUSHING
BAL-Moore 9–40, Hill 9–31, Unitas 6–30, Boyd 1–(-9)
CLE-Brown 27–114, Green 10–29, Ryan 3–2, Warfield 1–(-3)

PASSING
BAL-Unitas 12–20–2–95
CLE-Ryan 11–18–1–206

RECEIVING
BAL-Berry 3–38, Lorick 3–18, Orr 2–31, Moore 2–4, Hill 1–2, Mackey 1–2
CLE-Collins 5–130, Brown 3–37, Brewer 2–25, Warfield 1–13

#1

BROWNS 30, LOS ANGELES RAMS 28
DECEMBER 24, 1950

Everything Old Is New Again

Finally, after decades of frustration, Cleveland had a championship professional football team. And within a month, that team left town—perhaps serving as an ominous portent for events to come.

The Cleveland Rams hadn't garnered much attention from area sports fans during their nine-year existence, primarily because they were rarely competitive. But when they got over the hump, they went all the way, capturing the 1945 NFL championship with a thrilling one-point victory over the Washington Redskins in the title game at Cleveland Stadium. But even before the players had spent their bonus money, Rams owner Dan Reeves announced he was moving the team to Los Angeles, making the Rams the first West Coast squad in American professional sports.

Cleveland was left without a team—a championship team, no less—but few seemed to care. There was already quite a buzz about a new pro football team starting up led by former Massillon and Ohio State coach Paul Brown that would generate more interest from Cleveland sports fans in one year than the Rams did in nine. While the Rams struggled to stay above .500 in Los Angeles through the rest of the 1940s, the Browns dominated the All-American Football Conference and earned an invitation to join the NFL when the AAFC folded after the 1949 campaign. While the Browns introduced the established league to their new-age style of play and rolled to the title game in their first season, the Rams were following a similar script in California.

Splitting quarterback duties between future Hall of Famers Norm Van Brocklin and Bob Waterfield (who had played with the Rams in Cleveland), the Rams created football's first dominant passing game. The Los Angeles offense was unstoppable in 1950, scoring a touchdown on every fourteenth play and averaging nearly forty points per contest while setting twenty-two league records. Van Brocklin and Waterfield had combined for a whopping 3,600 passing yards and twenty-nine touchdown passes—utterly outrageous numbers for the time period. On the strength of its electric offensive attack, the Rams went 9–3 and sprinted past the Chicago Bears in a tie-breaking playoff to earn a trip to the title game. They would return to Cleveland for the first time since capturing the championship five years before. It was, Brown would say, "a fiction writer's delight."

While the Cleveland offense had been dynamic in its inaugural NFL season, it paled next to that of Los Angeles. The 1950 title would be decided by the Cleveland defense, which had been the best in football and was decidedly stronger than the Rams'. The only way the Browns' offense could keep up was if their defense could slow down the Los Angeles express.

Thus, the stage was set for one of the most incredible championship games in the history of sports, played in a remarkably dramatic setting: Christmas Eve afternoon along the polar landscape of Lake Erie.

Though the frigid temperature would affect attendance for the game, the Browns had already established the solid fan base the Rams never had. "For the first time in the history of professional football in Cleveland," Gordon Cobbledick wrote, "they have developed a solid core of followers. . . . The people who attend the Browns games now (and they're pretty much the same people week after week) have 'bought' professional football. It's reasonable to suppose their number will grow as the years roll by. The day when Cleveland was known as a one-sport town has passed."

It was a watershed moment in Cleveland sports history: the old team versus the new team with everything on the line. With an incredible eleven future Hall of Fame players participating, the contest more than lived up to expectations, unfolding like a storybook.

The Rams' dominant offense took center stage on the very first play. Twenty-seven seconds into the contest, the Rams cleverly used their primary receivers—Tom Fears and Elroy Hirsch—as decoys, and Waterfield streaked a pass down the sideline for tailback Glenn Davis, who reeled it in and motored untouched for an 82-yard touchdown and a 7–0 Rams lead. The Browns bounced back with a quick six-play, 72-yard drive capped by an Otto Graham–to–Dub Jones scoring pass to tie the game. But eight plays later, the Rams surged back ahead on a short Dick Hoerner touchdown run. The two explosive offenses had combined for three touchdowns in the game's first fifteen plays from scrimmage.

Though the pace of the scoring slowed, the potency of the offenses did not. On their ensuing possession, the Browns methodically drove down the field and scored on a Graham–to–Dante Lavelli pass. A bad center snap cost the Browns the extra point, and the Rams hung onto the lead at 14–13. The shell-shocked Cleveland defense gradually awoke, halting one Los Angeles drive inside the Browns ten yard line with an interception then stiffening on another that ended with a missed field goal. Leading the defensive charge was end Len Ford, playing in his first game in nearly three months after being sidelined for half the season with a broken jaw and dropping nearly twenty-five pounds while on an all-liquid diet.

Buoyed by their defense, the Browns started the second half with momentum and took their first lead on another Lavelli touchdown reception, capping a slick 77-yard march to make it 20–14. But as the third quarter progressed, the tide of momentum turned in the Rams' favor with a pair of touchdowns in a twenty-five-second period. First, after a long Waterfield pass set the Rams up at the Cleveland seventeen, Hoerner carried the football seven straight times before plowing over from the three yard line to put L.A. ahead again. Then, on the Browns' next play, Marion Motley was caught in the backfield and fumbled at his own six, where Rams defensive end Larry Brink scooped up the loose ball and rumbled into the end zone to make it 28–20. The Browns were on the ropes.

But, as they'd done all season, they responded to adversity. Early in the fourth quarter, defensive back Warren Lahr picked off Waterfield, and then Graham converted on a pair of critical fourth-down situations before hitting a diving Rex Bumgardner from nineteen yards out to cut the margin to 28–27 with ten minutes remaining. The Cleveland defense rose to the occasion and stymied Los Angeles on three plays, setting the table for more of Graham's heroics. The Browns drove to the Rams thirty-one yard line with three minutes left and were poised to take the lead when Graham rumbled for a 7-yard gain to the twenty-four. But, as he fought for extra yardage, Graham was blasted by linebacker Milan Lazetich and fumbled the football. Lazetich recovered it, and Graham returned to the sideline despondent. "I wanted to dig a hole right in the middle of that stadium, crawl into it and bury myself forever," he said later. "I wanted to die right there." Brown, not exactly known to try to make players feel better about themselves, told Graham not to worry. The Browns would get the ball back and figure out a way to win the game.

Appropriately, it would be up to the league's best defense to give the team one last chance. The Browns' front wall stuffed Hoerner for no gain on first down, then permitted nothing on another Hoerner rush on the next snap. On third-and-ten, Davis squirted through a hole over right tackle and found daylight but was dragged down four yards short of a first down. The Rams were forced to punt, and Cliff Lewis returned a booming 51-yard Waterfield kick thirteen yards to the Cleveland thirty-two, where Graham took the field again with 1:50 remaining.

As nightfall approached, Graham scrambled for fourteen yards, then connected on three straight passes—thirteen yards to Bumgardner, sixteen yards to Dub Jones, and twelve more to Bumgardner. With the clock ticking under thirty seconds, Graham took the fifth snap of the drive and positioned the football in the middle of the field at the Los Angeles eleven. Paul Brown called on Lou Groza to give the Browns their first NFL championship.

The image would be frozen into Cleveland history: Hal Herring's snap was perfect, Tommy James's hold was precise. The mammoth Groza took two powerful steps forward and kicked the football like a missile over the mass of humanity wrestling before him. The ball sailed through the gunmetal sky and swirling Lake Erie wind and split the uprights, carrying three rows into the Stadium bleachers with twenty-eight seconds remaining. That moment, wrote the *Plain Dealer*'s Harry Jones, "may well be the greatest gridiron spectacle in Cleveland history."

A last-gasp Los Angeles drive ended when Lahr picked off Van Brocklin at the Cleveland ten. As time expired, thousands of fans rushed the field to celebrate Cleveland's third professional football championship, but more importantly, the first for their beloved Browns.

It was everything a championship game could be. The teams combined for more than 800 total yards, forty-four first downs, eight touchdowns, and—a sign of things to come—sixty-five pass attempts and forty completions. And with a spellbinding comeback capped by an unforgettable climax, the 1950 NFL Championship ensured its place in history as one of the finest ever played. "There was never a game like this one," Paul Brown observed afterward.

Nor a grander statement made by the new kids on the block. "The Browns at long last have proven they can play with the big boys in the National League," Harold Sauerbrei wrote. After being told to "go get a football" upon their founding in 1945, Sauerbrei added, the Browns "now have left no shred of doubt that they are the masters of all football."

A distinction made in almost rhapsodic terms. The new had beaten the old, and Cleveland's love affair with the Browns was cast in a metallic mold that would prove unbreakable.

"This was a story that the people in Hollywood would reject as preposterous if submitted for a movie," Sauerbrei wrote in Monday's *Plain Dealer*. "And if you believe in Santa Claus this Christmas morning, you can believe the story that unfolded."

	1	2	3	4	
Rams	14	0	14	0	=28
Browns	7	6	7	10	=30

First Quarter

LA-Davis 82-yd. pass from Waterfield (Waterfield kick)

CLE-Jones 31-yd. pass from Graham (Groza kick)

LA-Hoerner 3-yd. run (Waterfield kick)

Second Quarter

CLE-Lavelli 26-yd. pass from Graham (Groza kick)

Third Quarter

CLE-Lavelli 39-yd. pass from Graham (Groza kick)

LA-Hoerner 1-yd. run (Waterfield kick)

LA-Brink 6-yd. fumble return (Waterfield kick)

Fourth Quarter

CLE-Bumgardner 19-yd. pass from Graham (Groza kick)

CLE-Groza 16-yd. FG

RUSHING

CLE-Graham 12–99, Motley 6–9, Jones 2–4, Bumgardner 5–2, Lavelli 1–2

PASSING

CLE-Graham 22–32–1–298, Jones 0–1–0–0

RECEIVING

CLE-Lavelli 11–128, Jones 4–80, Bumgardner 4–46, Gillom 1–29, Speedie 1–17, Motley 1–(-2)